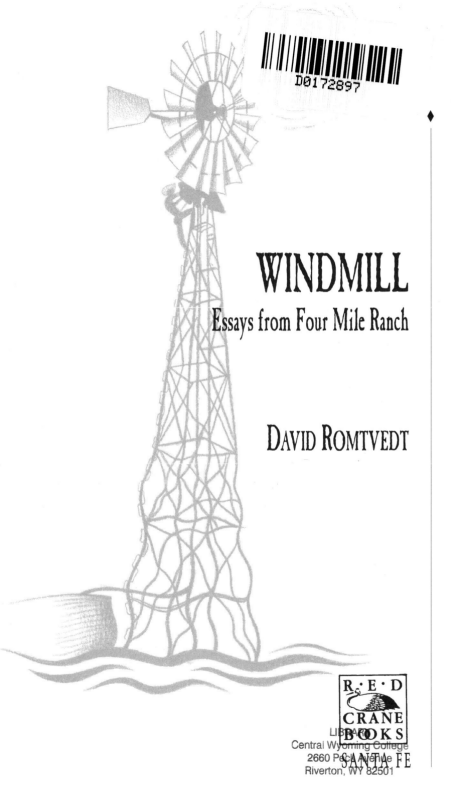

WINDMILL
Essays from Four Mile Ranch

DAVID ROMTVEDT

R · E · D
CRANE
BOOKS
SANTA FE

for my father-in-law
Simon Iberlin
with gratitude and love

♦ ♦ ♦

FIRST EDITION
Manufactured in the United States of America
Cover painting and interior illustrations by Gregory Truett Smith
Book design and production by Beverly Miller Atwater

Library of Congress Cataloging-in-Publication Data
Romtvedt, David.
    Windmill : essays from Four Mile Ranch/David Romtvedt.—1st ed.
        p.   cm.
    ISBN 1-878610-62-7 (alk. paper)
    1. Romtvedt, David—Homes and haunts—Wyoming—Buffalo.
2. Buffalo Region (Wyo.)—Social life and customs. 3. Basque Americans—Wyoming—Buffalo—History. 4. Authors, American—20th century—Biography. 5. Ranch life—Wyoming—Buffalo. 6. Ranchers—Wyoming—Biography.   I. Title.
PS3568.05655Z473   1997
814'.54—dc21
                                                    96-29729
                                                    CIP

Red Crane Books
2008-B Rosina Street
Santa Fe, NM 87505
http://www.redcrane.com
email: publish@redcrane.com

Contents

Also by David Romtvedt:

Certainty
Crossing Wyoming
A Flower Whose Name I Do Not Know
How Many Horses
Free and Compulsory for All
Moon

Editor with Dollie Iberlin, *Buffalotarrak: An Anthology of the Basque People of Buffalo, Wyoming.*

Acknowledgments

"Culture" appeared in the *Casper Star-Tribune*.

"Day of Rest" appeared in *The Sun*.

"Simon," under the title "With Simon at Four Mile Ranch," appeared in *Buffalotarrak: An Anthology of the Basque People of Buffalo, Wyoming* (Red Hills Publications, 1995).

"Strange Communion: Notes of a Non-Hunter" is reprinted with permission of *Orion*. It appeared in Vol. 15 no. 1, (Winter 1996). The quotation in that chapter from *The Stars, the Snow, the Fire* by John Haines is reprinted with the permission of Graywolf Press.

The author would like to thank Kate Camino and Dollie Iberlin for their assistance in the writing of this book.

The Windmill

I pull on the dark coveralls and climb the delicate ladder.
At the top I pull myself onto the narrow platform
and clip the heavy safety harness around the steel shaft.
I take a wrench from my pocket and remove the tin plate
covering the oil pan. The cogged wheels rest, partially
submerged in their bath of graying oil. I drain this oil
into a bucket and lower it with a rope to the ground.
As I pour in fresh oil the wind rises. Though the rotor
blades are locked they try to turn and the assembly
swings around threatening to knock me into space.
I lean against the mill and pour. The wind catches
the stream of oil making it fly in long looping threads.
Where it lands it will kill the grass. Back on earth
I release the brake and the blades spin, singing in the wind.
The water spills into the stock tank. It is pure and clear,
and so, gratefully, I cup my greasy hands and drink.

Sheepwagon ♦

These pages have been written in a sheepwagon behind our house in Buffalo, Wyoming. Once this sheepwagon was a daily part of the work of my Basque father-in-law Simon Iberlin's Four Mile Ranch. Now it's a writer's office and summer guest cottage filled with romance. The stories I tell here are in no chronological order and, though they are based on the work I do at Four Mile, they will not teach anyone how to be a rancher.

When I leave our house, the sheepwagon and the town of Buffalo, I go to Four Mile. At the ranch, I've fixed fence, moved cows, searched for missing horses, winter-fed stock, vaccinated, castrated and branded calves, helped neighbors with sheep shearing and docking and, above all else, maintained and repaired windmills. As I've worked at Four Mile, I've thought about the changes that have come both to this ranch and to ranching generally. That means I've thought a lot about loss.

Once as I was changing the oil in the running gear of the

Rickett's Field windmill, I saw a rotting sheepwagon laid over on its side halfway up the ridgeline. The wagon's running gear had long ago been stripped away and only the ribs that had supported the rounded canvas roof were left. A few blackened shreds of canvas hung from the skeletal ribbing and flapped in the wind. The window glass was broken out and lay around the wagon reflecting shards of sunlight. Animals had walked through the wagon and what once had been a side wall was now a floor covered by bits of clay, straw and manure. Before its decline, this sheepwagon had been some solitary herder's home, a refuge from late winter storms, an essential part of sheep ranching.

A few sheepwagons are still in service on ranches but most are either falling apart or, like mine in Buffalo, parked somewhere, doing some other job. One way of life is disappearing as another comes into view. Whatever I feel about that, I know that the sheepwagon will still be here. Even the rotting one in Rickett's Field will take a hundred years or more to disintegrate.

Though I don't live at Four Mile Ranch, I often stay the night there after work. Sometimes it's too late to get back to town, sometimes I just want to stay. The ranch house is a two-room cabin with a wood cookstove in the kitchen and a potbellied stove in the bedroom. The cabin has no electricity, no running water. There's a cistern filled by rain coming off the corrugated tin roof of the shearing barn. There's an outhouse next to the coal shed. Because black widow spiders make their home in the outhouse, we keep a broom by the door and sweep the area before we enter.

When I stay at the ranch, I sleep in the cabin, or in a cottonwood grove beside a horseshoe bend Four Mile Creek

makes a half mile east of the cabin. As the creek is normally dry, it is a monument to the stream's tenacity that it has managed to form this deep U from spring floodwaters alone. Looking up through the cottonwood trees, I see clouds and sky, and I feel much farther from town than the forty miles I drive to get here.

Sometimes I sleep out alone. Sometimes my family is with me—my wife Margo and daughter Caitlin, my nephew Matthew who spends much of his time with us, and my parents-in-law Simon and Dollie. In winter the nighttime temperature drops to ten, twenty, thirty, forty below zero. In the uninsulated cabin it's impossible to sleep through the night without getting up to feed the stove. We go to sleep with a raging fire and a temperature of eight-five. We wake in the night and it's twenty-six degrees in the room.

Before World War Two, which was before widespread fencing, the herders who worked here and on the mountain would often spend most of their nights awake. They'd come out of their sheepwagons and stare into the darkness, singing and shouting to keep coyotes away from the sheep. They'd fire rifle shots into the sky. They'd walk around the bands of sleeping sheep, banging a burlap bag soaked in kerosene on the ground to make an olfactory fence. A fence like this wouldn't stop a coyote, but on reaching the ring of kerosene smell the dog would stop for a moment and sniff. That gave the Border collies enough time to bark, and the herders enough time to shoot.

As spring approached and the days began to warm up, the herders would peel off their long underwear, sometimes for the first time in several months.

My father-in-law Simon said to me, "You know those

undergarments would be pretty ripe by the end of March. At lambing time we'd just pile them up around the sheep. That was about the best thing to keep a coyote away."

The interior of my sheepwagon is twelve feet long by just over six feet wide. There is a door slightly off center at one end of the wagon. When you step in, there is a cast-iron woodstove to your right. The stove is both for heat and for cooking. Against the wall near the stove are shelves and cupboards with latches like those on a sailboat. When you move sheep, you also move your sheepwagon. The latched cupboards hold everything in place.

At the far end of the wagon from the doorway is a raised bed. This bed is very comfortable for one person and bearable for two people who get along. The length of the bed is the width of the wagon. Beneath the bed is a pullout shelf which serves as a dining table, office desk and workbench. On this shelf I have a small laptop computer. On either side of the shelf is a bench against the sheepwagon wall. I sit at one bench. Across from me on the other bench sits a 24-pin printer.

An orange extension cord runs out through a crack in the door and around a flower bed I've planted outside the sheepwagon window. There are yellow and blue bearded iris, phlox and day lilies that undulate in the wind, impatiens, Shasta daisies, poppies, yarrow, monarda, cosmos, zinnia, columbine, statice and two flowers whose names I've never learned though they are perennials I nurture and greet fondly each spring when they return to life.

The extension cord runs across a short expanse of ground, through our garage and into a storage shed where it's plugged into an outlet that's part of the light fixture with a bare bulb hanging from the ceiling. In winter I must bring the computer into the house at night because of the cold. With a few sticks of wood, the stove will warm the sheepwagon nicely, but as with the cabin at the ranch you have to keep feeding the fire. And the sheepwagon stove is much smaller than the stove at the cabin so you have to get up several times in the night to keep the wagon from freezing. The computer literature warned me about leaving my laptop out at forty below. With coal, I could keep a fire going in the sheepwagon whether I'm sleeping there or not, but the smell of coal is awful and so I resist burning the black diamonds.

In winter, I move into the house, bringing the computer with me. I unplug the extension cord that in summer powers the computer and I plug this cord into the block heater of my 1975 Chevy van. In the deep cold, the orange cord becomes stiff as steel. Sometimes when I move it, it snaps in half. I patch it with black electrical tape.

Sheepwagons have many separate storage spaces. There's one at the outside under the rear window. It can hold firewood or jerry cans of water or tools. There's another space in front of each of the rear wheels of the wagon. These are smaller and useful for gloves, leather-working tools, bags of dried fruit. Inside the wagon, there are two large spaces beneath the bed, and two tall narrow ones underneath the benches. Extra bedding and heavy coats go in these. Even in a sheepwagon—one of the world's most compact homes—a person could gather a lot of possessions.

I have listened to herders tell of life sixty years ago, of lying down to sleep and gazing out their sheepwagon window onto a sky packed full of stars. Often, my wife Margo and I tire of our house in town with its sense of insulation from the world. Then we sleep in the wagon. We open the window next to the bed and the cool summer air blows across our faces. In winter we close the window as tightly as we can and burrow deep into a down comforter. In either season, when we awaken in the night, it is to same black sky the herders saw, the same stars.

I'm told that God speaks more openly in the presence of distance and silence. Even so, I must listen very carefully to hear God's voice. The silence of the sheepwagon helps me to hear.

There are two windows on either side of the wagon above the benches, and another window in the door. It is light and cheery inside, though when the wind blows, one might prefer having solid walls.

One June night as I was coming down out of the Bighorns with my friend John Lane, we saw a light we didn't recognize off to the northeast. UFOs maybe, or a giant city that had been built in our two-week absence from civilization. We stopped our truck and got out. In the stillness, we saw the Northern Lights—long shimmering bands of yellow and white pouring down from the top of the world, then racing back up.

We stared. After a few minutes, we heard the rumbling of thunder from the southeast, and, turning, we saw lightning—jagged fierce bolts, some running up and down, some back and forth across the sky. We turned from one light to the other.

Next came singing. It wasn't the long howling singing of wolves—the last Bighorn wolf was shot in 1939. Rather, it was the singing of coyotes—short bright yips very close to laughter. There were so many singers that the song took on a quality that seemed familiar, human.

Sheep need to be protected from coyotes but I can't help but feel sympathy for the clever dog. Coyote will find a way around every impediment—traps, poisons, guns, trucks, snowmobiles, airplanes. When night falls, no matter how hard the day, Coyote begins to sing. Coyote's song is "We are here; it is now."

In many parts of the world it has been considered an abomination to say God's name aloud. Such speech makes God flee. I think this God who flees from its name is the same God who won't shout at me. It's a very different God from the Christian one I was taught about in my childhood. That God was fierce and bold, warlike and angry, a man.

There is always a mask for God. This mask is a name and a presence whose name we can say aloud. One mask is Nature. But the mask is not the real God. The real God hesitates beyond the edge of speech.

On the mountain the coyotes' singing was both diffident and spirited. There were so many voices overlapping that the song arrived as flowing water tumbling down from the mountain over boulders and around sharp bends. The water could not be held within the banks of the river. The sound became a flood rising over the brushy banks and into the trees, making the leaves tremble, and finally disappearing into the sky. The sound carried everything with it, reminding us that we were all one.

When the coyotes quit singing, John and I got back in the truck, started the engine and drove down the mountain into town. The next day I went out to the sheepwagon to work and found I was just sitting there doing nothing. I felt as if the coyote song had come flowing down with the river and washed right through my sheepwagon. I opened the small door at the front of the wagon, opened the even smaller window at the back and watched the watery music stream out onto the ground. "No wonder I can't work," I said aloud. "My plastic and silicon computer has been sitting under coyote song water all night. My papers are stuck together and the ink has run together to form swirling dark clouds."

The current of song had carried huge boulders. One of these had been thrown straight through my doorway. It was as if the moon had been shot through a keyhole. The boulder had smashed into the stove and both the stove and the stone had been broken into many small pieces so that the two could not be told apart.

When my daughter Caitlin came out to call me in for lunch she noticed the mess on the floor which I'd thought was my business alone. She looked down and asked me, "What are you doing with all these beautiful little rocks, Dad?"

When I looked at her, her eyes sparkled and I saw that for one moment, thanks to an impossible natural event, the rift human beings have made in the universe was healed.

My daughter keeps pet snakes and lizards she brings into town from the ranch. Her favorite reptile, though, was a Painted turtle she found on the road east of our house and which she kept for a time as a pet. After several weeks, we decided it was time for the turtle to go home. I hooked the trailer up to my bike. Caitlin climbed in with the turtle on her lap. She buckled the seat belt and shoulder harness, trying to make sure that the turtle would be as secure as she was. I bicycled out of town to a spot where there was marshy boggy land along Clear Creek. I lifted Caitlin with the turtle in her arms over the inevitable barbed-wire fence. We walked across a long field and came down to the wetland. There we picked a likely spot—tall grasses, rocks along the bank, mud and debris, a few small shrubby trees along and in the water.

When we set the turtle down, it began to purposefully stride across the mud and grasses. It plunged into the slow-moving water near the bank, bobbing and drifting. It climbed back out onto soggy ground, then once more it headed for the water. This time it moved toward the main channel of the creek. It crossed a small gravel bar and kept going. At the tip of the bar, it entered the main current of the creek and spun wildly downstream. We ran along for thirty or forty yards watching the turtle struggle, sink, and rise to struggle again. Several times the force of the current spun it end over end. Then the turtle was gone. It had returned to its life, leaving ours behind.

The inside of my sheepwagon is sumptuous beyond anything the early herders knew. Running the length of the ceiling is a drying rack over which I hang wet towels and freshly laundered shirts. The curving interior of the roof, which also forms the side walls of the wagon, is covered with wallpaper—white with tiny mauve leaf shapes and even tinier dots. The woodwork is painted with white oil based enamel, gleaming and easy to clean. The benches are red enamel, equally easy to clean.

On the day before Thanksgiving, it was eighteen below. It stayed cold until December fourth when it warmed up and snowed thirty-six inches. The next morning was clear and brilliantly cold. I built a qhuinzee—a snow house—for the kids. Caitlin, my nephew Matthew and I went inside. We stuck a spoon in the wall, set a candle in the spoon and lit it.

The warmth from the candle made a tiny domed recess in the qhuinzee wall.

Inspired, the kids and I left the qhuinzee and spent the afternoon cross-country skiing in the pastures along Clear Creek. Around 4:30 as it grew dusky, I dropped Caitlin and Matthew at their grandparents' for dinner and I went home. When I stepped into the house it was silent. "Margo?" I called. Only the ticking of the clock on the kitchen wall answered me. Margo is a potter and the owner of a craft gallery. Though the gallery is several blocks away, her studio and kilns are right behind our house. I'm much more likely to find her in the studio than in the house and so I stepped through the empty rooms and opened the back door. "Margo?" I called again.

"Yes," her voice answered, coming not from the studio but from the sheepwagon. "Come out here."

I walked across the yard listening to the crunch of my boots on the dry snow. I banged the snow off on the hitch of the sheepwagon and stepped in. Margo had put a tablecloth over the shelf. The table was set. A long stemmed pale blue wineglass stood at each place. Candles were burning and the light gave the small space a burnished coppery glow. She invited me to sit down and we had dinner together. In the deep snow the world was as silent as the empty house. The fire in the stove really did chuckle. I opened the window behind me and felt the icy breeze. Inside the wagon we were safe and warm. After dinner we climbed up on the bed and lay down together, listening to the stillness.

In June a couple of years ago it rained nearly every day for over two weeks. "We haven't had rain like this in fifty years," Simon told me. A visitor wondered if she had somehow gotten turned around and found herself not in Wyoming but in Ireland.

Each morning that June I lit a fire in the sheepwagon. The rain rattled on the curved metal roof. It was hard to regulate the temperature in the wagon. Two or three sticks of wood sent it up to ninety degrees, then when the fire died down, it quickly dropped into the forties. I kept opening and closing the door. Each time I opened it, I'd stand there for a few minutes staring at the grass, wondering how anything could be so green. There was more green outside my door than is usual in the entire state.

A few miles east, in the Powder River Breaks, the land remained dry in spite of so much rain nearby. Breaks are by definition rugged, heavily eroded, scarred by ravines and gullies, largely devoid of human activity, and, above all else, dry.

The rain clouds come down off the face of the mountains spent and stupefied by their climb to over 13,000 feet. They drop what little water is left to them over the town of Buffalo then drift over the Breaks as if that harsh landscape were invisible.

In a sense, this is true. Each ridge in the Breaks is like a knife blade shoved deep into the sky. Standing on one ridgeline, it is impossible to see into the ravine behind the next ridge. A thousand men could be resting there, chatting and waiting for their work to begin, and from a hundred yards away there would be no evidence of their existence. Such land is practiced at hiding its guests.

When I am out in the Breaks, I am filled by their emptiness, their lonely beauty. It is strange to me that most people find the Breaks inhospitable and raw. Visitors tell me the terrain is ugly. If the visitors are kind and articulate, they pause when I look expectantly at them. Then they tell me, "It's an austere place." I admit that it's the kind of landscape a developer might be interested in only as a last resort for those who have already visited the earth's scenic wonders and now have nowhere else to go.

I give thanks to Four Mile Ranch which, in human terms, provides the land with purpose and protection. The ranch, by defining the level of human use, keeps most human intrusion away. This includes even the intrusion that is our family for though my father-in-law Simon lived on the ranch as a boy and young man, he has for many years now lived in town. He and his wife Dollie have a big rambling well-lived-in house only a few blocks from ours. When we go to work, Simon and I get in the pickup and commute.

One of the forces that drove many people to town was the need for schooling. It was impossible for people to get their children into town during the winter and so some families moved in for the school season. Other families boarded their children with town people during the school year. Simon's brother John Iberlin bought a small house in town and his boys lived there on their own to attend high school. John and his wife Maggie stayed on their ranch Wormwood which borders Four Mile to the southeast. On weekends and during school vacations, John and Maggie's boys were back at the ranch.

The boys' experience of living alone for school traced in reverse the experience of the Basque sheepherders who came to the Bighorn Mountain region. Those first sheepherders often lived alone for a year, or two, or three in a sheepwagon. In winter they followed the sheep far from the mountains out onto untilled rangeland. In June after lambing and docking, the herder and sheepwagon followed the sheep back up the mountains to summer pasture. Nowadays many sheep are trucked up the mountain. The stock-rests along the trail as you come up from open country are still there but they're much less used.

For years our sheepwagon has been almost nowhere but behind our house. In early August it rolls down Main Street in the County Fair and Rodeo Parade. On August fifteenth, when there is a parade to honor the Basque settlers of Johnson County and northern Wyoming, it rolls again, this time with many other sheepwagons down the same Main Street.

It seems appropriate that I who have moved so many times would work in a sheepwagon—a house on wheels. Born in Portland, Oregon, I lived there off and on during my first seven years. With my family I also lived in the Oregon towns of Jennings Lodge, Gladstone, Bandon, and Coquille, and on a farm near the small town of Bonanza in the Langell Valley. During the summer I turned eight, my family moved to Arizona and I lived in Goodyear, Avondale, Phoenix and Tucson. I attended six different elementary schools. After high school, I returned to Oregon for college then to graduate school in Iowa and Texas, the Peace Corps in Zaire and Rwanda, finally settling in Washington where I lived in Olympia and Port Townsend.

These were my homes; I've left out traveling. In my past, each town, city or chunk of ground was more a backdrop to life than a life itself. In this way, I came to Wyoming unsure what it was to belong to a place. I was not so much unhappy as a result of the vagabond trajectory I'd followed as simply blind to the dictates of land and to the gift the land can make of itself.

When my wife Margo returns home from even a short

trip away from Wyoming, she stops her car at the border. She steps out and begins to walk away from the road—usually into open prairie and sage grassland, sometimes into high desert or mountains. Away from the road and from other people, she lies face down on the ground and cries. Her tears disappear into the grass. She tells me that her feeling is part ecstasy and part sorrow. It is the feeling of belonging to what is not human, and having it belong to you.

I once worked as a writer-in-residence in Turner, Montana, a small town on the Montana Highline near the Saskatchewan border. The entire high school had thirty-six students. These young people had known each other all of their lives. All of the people in Turner had known each other all of their lives.

The students spoke to me openly and unselfconsciously about topics many people can only make fun of or avoid— sex and drugs, finding a place in society, parents and neighbors, racism, the possibility of nuclear holocaust or environmental collapse, their own deepest feelings.

I thought belonging somewhere must make you grow up faster. Then I realized that nearly all of these young people would leave Turner when they finished high school. One of their deepest hopes was to escape the community which had made them. Most of them planned to never return.

Here in Buffalo, Wyoming, the young long to leave their home, too. They begin early in their lives dreaming and scheming ways to get out of here. Most of them find it difficult to imagine how one could live in this little backward spot with no possibilities for advancement, no outlet for ambition. Those who were born and raised here and want to stay must confront the unspoken assumption that whoever stays must be somehow deficient—too weak or stupid or complacent to make it in the larger world outside of our town. Many adults believe this of themselves.

Nowadays people rarely say where they are from, or where they live. Instead, they say something like, "I'm based in Santa Clara." As if everyone were a recruit in a great industrial army whose generals might mobilize the forces at any moment.

Or people say, "She's out of Austin." As if she were playing basketball in the NBA and had been drafted from the University of Texas.

When people speak in this way, they mean that they live in these places but they are not of them. They don't say, "I live in Buffalo, Wyoming." They are based in Buffalo. And any minute now they won't be.

When I moved to Wyoming, I joked that the state had basically the same climate as Arizona where I'd grown up. When people asked how I was adapting to Wyoming, I'd say, "Oh, fine, it's the same climate as Arizona—just a hundred degrees cooler at any given moment."

It is cold here and much of Wyoming looks like the desert but the feeling is unlike any other place I've been. The dark forbidding enclosure of the cold, the distance and separation people experience because they must insulate themselves from winter. It often seems to me that people insulate themselves from each other. They wait quietly in their houses, staring out the windows at the wind driven snow, the ice growing downward from the eaves. In town, they step outside to shovel snow off their sidewalks, to plow out their drives. In the country, they take the same steps outside to check on sheep and cattle. People seem so isolated. But that is only surface.

I now think I have misunderstood. What I have seen as "insulation," as withholding and denial of feeling, may be to those who have always lived here and who know this life simply a way to show respect, to honor privacy. There is a comfort and dignity that people gain through restraint.

I notice that when one person needs help, another offers help. Neither party reminds the other of this. People just help. To speak of it would demean everyone as it would taint the act of helping.

In writing about Buffalo, Wyoming, and the people who live here, I want to honor both. I fear, though, that any words at all will not so much honor as diminish northern Wyoming. Speaking may be a way to deny the integrity of both the land and its people. This is the risk I take as a writer and as a newcomer, a person who, having lived here only twelve years, seeks to tell Buffalo's story.

To know this land, one must embrace its silence, its forbidden heart, its secrets. But these secrets are not really so secret. They lie open as an empty field. They are uninterested in our longing, uninterested in being secrets. It is only we—only I—who make them what they are not.

The sheepwagon rocks in the wind. Like the place and its residents, it is without guile, without pretense. The high northern plains and the mountains call out. The call is enticing, and from inside the sheepwagon, I listen.

Buffalo

♦

B uffalo is the county seat of Johnson County in north
central Wyoming. The town lies at 4,645 feet above sea
level. Though that's close to a mile up, it's a low eleva-
tion for Wyoming. If we were to descend to sea level, we'd
still be over a thousand horizontal miles away from the
Pacific ocean. To reach Buffalo, rain clouds from the West
must climb the Coast Ranges of Oregon and the Olympic
Mountains of Washington, then the Cascades, the Rockies
and, finally, our own easternmost thrust of the Rockies, the
Bighorns. By the time these rain clouds reach us, there's not
much water left to drop. The same is true of clouds from the
south which must travel nearly two thousand miles from the
Gulf of Mexico.

In Johnson County, and throughout Wyoming, water is
rare. Our yearly precipitation is about thirteen inches. Not
much rain and not much snow. People say that it snows a
foot in October, then that snow blows around till it wears out
eight months later. In summer, day after day dawns clear and

dry, then one day in August it can rain two inches in thirty minutes. Or hail falls in rocklike lumps. In either case, the sun-hardened earth is unable to allow any water in and so it runs off washing what little topsoil we have into the sandy streambeds. Ours is a small landlocked town in a large landlocked state—97,914 square miles of basin and range.

Buffalo rests at the base of the Bighorn Mountains. At 13,175 feet, Cloud Peak is the highest mountain in the range. The mountain knows no water will come to it and so it has gone to the water that hangs above it in the sky.

In spring, this water runs down off the mountains, at the very base of which is a series of well-watered ranches. Irrigation ditches snake along the edges of meadowlike fields. Great metal sprinklers roll across the terrain like ancient armies. Ranchers put up ton after ton of hay. Buffalo sits placidly, surrounded by these ranches.

The Buffalo I live in is a Basque community made up largely of ranchers, though in my generation many Basques have given up ranching for the ambiguous pleasures of town. About three hundred of Buffalo's three thousand inhabitants claim Basque heritage. Most of the three hundred are related to me by marriage.

Of the ranching Basques, both past and present, few have ranched the well-watered slopes of the Bighorns. As you move away from town and away from the mountains, you find dryland ranches. These are the ranches that are run by Basques. As the amount of live water gets smaller, the ranches get larger—25,000, 35,000, 60,000, 90,000 acres.

At my father-in-law Simon Iberlin's Four Mile Ranch there are nearly 35,000 acres with no running water. There are creek beds where, fifty years ago, water flowed, at least seasonally. Cottonwood trees line these watercourses, but there's no water in them. For water, we have windmills—nineteen windmills which regularly break down and must be fixed as they are the source of all the water we provide to cattle and sheep. The wild animals drink this water, too, and, because they could not survive without this water, I think our responsibility to them is as great as it is to the domestic stock.

I first encountered windmills when I began to work at Four Mile. Before this, I'd known of windmills mostly from Don Quixote's tilting. As I came to know real working windmills, I also came to know the stubborn and powerful people from the Pyrenees—the Basques. I hadn't completely left Don Quixote behind.

A man who retired to Buffalo told me that shortly after he had moved to town, he was working in his yard when a woman drove up across the street.

"She parked her little red car, got out and went in the house across from mine," the man told me. "Later, she came out, got back in the car and drove away. The next day I was working in the yard again when the woman returned, but this time, after parking her car, she got out and walked straight toward me, smiling and waving her hand. I turned and looked behind me, you know like in the movies, thinking there must be someone there she knew. When I figured out she was waving at me, I walked toward her. We met in the middle of the street and stood there. She was a stocky woman with close-cropped hair and a broad smile. She thrust her hand toward mine and introduced herself, 'Hi. I'm Madeleine Harriet. Iberlin's my maiden name. That's my mother Jeanne Iberlin's house across the street. My brother

Simon Iberlin lives just up the block there, and down two houses is my other brother John Iberlin though John lives on the ranch and only uses the house when he has to be in town. My husband and I live just at the end of the street. I'm pleased to meet you and if you need anything, you just let any of us know. If we're not at home, we'll be on the mountain with the sheep.' Then she turned, walked back across the street and into her mother's house. I tell you, I was impressed."

The man shook his head in awe but didn't tell me exactly what it was that had impressed him. Maybe it was Madeleine's friendliness and what it suggested about small-town openness. Or maybe it was her solid approach and confident speech. Or maybe it was the fact that his neighbor, Madeleine's mother, was ninety-eight years old and still maintained her own large vegetable garden. Or maybe it was the sudden knowledge that he'd moved into a village compound in which most of the houses were inhabited by members of one Basque family. Or maybe it was that the entire conversation had taken place while the two stood in the middle of the street.

◆

The Basque homeland lies on both the north and south sides of the Pyrenees mountains rising up from the Bay of Biscay. The crest of the mountains now marks an imaginary line that is the border between France and Spain. Three of the seven Basque provinces are on land currently ruled by France. The remaining four provinces have fallen under the rule of Spain.

For thousands of years the Basque homeland—Euskadi in the Basque language—has been coveted by foreign powers.

It's been estimated that in their entire history, the Basque people have experienced national independence for less than a hundred years. Still, the Basques have retained a national identity separate from the Roman, French and Spanish people who have attempted to rule Euskadi. And wherever they have traveled, the Basques have maintained an identity separate from that of the other peoples amongst whom they live.

In the Basque country a family's land and property is traditionally left to the eldest child—male or female. Even in good times, this encouraged second, third, fourth and fifth children to leave home seeking their fortune.

Long before the official "discovery" of America, Basques had crossed the Atlantic as fishermen. In the fifteenth and sixteenth centuries, many of these fishermen, already skilled at finding their way in the vast oceans, became navigators on the ships exploring the New World. The feverish captains, admirals and adventurers, the desperate and hungry sailors, all those seeking gold or silver or freedom, turned to their Basque navigators and asked, "Where are we?"

The Basque navigators leaned into the trade winds. They stared intently at the stars and read the silent messages left on the dark sky. They gazed at the rolling waves, noticing at what point each wave broke, and in what direction. They spoke to God. Then they turned back to their captains and said only, "Farther."

As Spanish power was consolidated in much of the Americas, the Basques became central in the shipping industry, developing a monopoly relationship with the Spanish crown. Everything that came or went between the colonies and Spain meant profit to the Basque shippers. Only later was tax paid to the Spanish government.

Of the emigrant Basques who didn't become business-men, many became missionary priests or nuns. In 1527, the Basque Juan de Zumárraga was named Bishop of New Spain. And in 1534, the Basque Ignatius of Loyola founded the Jesuit Order.

During the sixteenth, seventeenth and eighteenth centuries, Basques were known in Europe as mercenaries, missionaries, mariners and merchants. Ironically, this powerful Basque presence in the colonial government and church has been somewhat obscured in the historical record because of the Spanish practice of listing Basques as simply citizens of Spain.

After the independence of Spain's colonies, newly independent governments often rejected what they saw as Basque interference. The Basque ruling elite was driven out of the new nations. The next round of Basque emigrants—those who came to North America—were among the poorer Basques. They left Europe, as many non-Basque people did, seeking work of any kind. Like their earlier more powerful brethren, these immigrants have been hidden from historical view. Immigration records in the New World countries listed the Basques not as coming from Euskadi but as from their place of national origin—Spain or France.

Both the Basques who made themselves an indispensable part of Spain's colonial government, and the later struggling immigrants seeking a new life, wandered the world, spreading themselves thinly over great expanses of North and South America.

Before they came to the Pyrenees and the Bay of Biscay, the Basque people may have lived in a land more like Wyoming, a land far from the sea. In their language—Euskara—

the oldest words—stone, soil, meadow, moss, tree, forest, cliff—are those of a mountain people. But these words could have come from the Basque life in the Pyrenees as well as from some earlier life in other mountains. No one really knows the origin of the Basque people.

♦

Jean Esponda was the first Basque to settle in Wyoming. His journey though was a roundabout one. In 1884, Esponda left his home in St. Etienne de Baigorry. Baigorry is in the province of Banafarroa, Euskadi, the province whose name the French have translated to Basse Navarre, in the region known in France as the Pays Basque.

From Baigorry, Esponda went to California where he worked for seventeen years. In California, he learned about sheep and he learned about America—that is to say he learned about making money, how easy it had been in the early days, how much harder it was now. In his first years as a herder, he took his wages not in cash but in sheep. When he had enough sheep he quit herding for other men and set off with the sheep he now owned, making use of the open range for grazing land and for water.

Like most Basques in this period, Esponda had no desire to become an American. He wanted only to make money, save it all and return to Euskadi a wealthy man. And so he worked hard. By 1901, the open range was disappearing in California. More and more fences crossed and cut the land. To graze sheep or cattle, a man had to have a deed. The days when anything might happen seemed to be over. To Jean Esponda, it now looked as if this continent was no longer a book of blank pages waiting to be written upon.

Deciding both that he was rich enough and that there was little hope of getting any richer, Esponda sold his sheep and went home to the Basque country where he hired workmen to build a splendid large house in which he would live the life of a wealthy retired gentleman. His was the homecoming of a successful emigrant returned. He wore new black trousers and a hat never touched by rain or snow. He drank from crystal glasses. But he wasn't happy and after six months he admitted to himself that the Basque country was no longer home, that he longed for California.

Turning his newly built house over to his family, Esponda took a steamer back to the east coast of the United States. From there, he took a train west. Alone, he rode silently as the changing landscape flashed past. The long miles piled up behind him as he left the Atlantic behind. He heard the clickety-clack, clickety-clack of the steel wheels on the rail joints, and he listened intently, as though to a language. He stared out the window.

Like most Basques, Esponda was a man of some restraint. He kept his feelings largely to himself. In his letters, he gave the news and little more. I often wonder what he thought both about his own life and about the large events of his day. His life and those events are my history, and history, I think, is the fiction that we agree upon, the illusion we seek to recover when we look behind us.

Esponda's departure from California and his return to Euskadi show that the Basque gentleman knew that this continent was changing irrevocably. But whether he saw this change as cruel destruction of a natural world and of the people who inhabited that world, or as economic development, necessary and perhaps even good, is impossible to say. We only know that he was disappointed in his return home and chose once again to leave for America, for some unspoken promise.

On the trip west from Chicago the ex-California sheep-man began to talk with a fellow traveler, Mr. Patsy Healy. To Healy, Esponda was simply another immigrant looking for work. It was the immigrant's good fortune that Healy was a partner in Healy and Patterson, the largest sheep operation in northeastern Wyoming. Esponda listened as Mr. Healy explained the sheep business in the new country—in Johnson County, Wyoming. Esponda learned that there were opportunities there for a man who was ready to work. The open range was disappearing but that presented possibility as well as loss. The new ranching industry would include irrigated hay fields, barbed wire fencing of those fields, privately owned winter pastures and winter feeding of stock. There would be room for more independent operators and for more herders. "And," Healy added, "if a man already knows English, he's that much ahead."

As the train rumbled forward, the two men kept up their conversation. When the train stopped in Buffalo, and Patsy Healy stepped down from the carriage, Jean Esponda stepped down, too. It was 1902 and Jean Esponda had become the first Basque to immigrate to Wyoming.

Esponda held his hand up to shade his eyes. He could see the Bighorns and, turning, he could see the earth opening out to the east. It was a land of space and sky and sage. Jean saw the ranching potential in this emptiness. He wrote home and encouraged his brother John to come to Wyoming. In a few months John arrived and saw, even more clearly than his brother Jean, that this was a land where a man might have great success. Only recently it had been a land of blood, the watercourses flowing red with the violent accumulation of the last forty years of the nineteenth century.

At first there were the battles to destroy the native peoples. General Sheridan, for whom the largest town in northern Wyoming is named, is the father of that immortal phrase, "The only good Indian is a dead Indian." Sheridan's superior, General Sherman, wrote, "We must act with vindictive earnestness against the Sioux, even to their extermination, men, women and children. Nothing else will reach the root of this case." In a letter to his brother John, Sherman said of Indians in general: "The more we can kill this year, the less will have to be killed in the next war." Another officer, Colonel John Chivington, an elder of the Methodist Church who had been a traveling preacher in Colorado's mining camps, ordered his troopers before the massacre at Sand Creek to "kill and scalp all, big and little; nits make lice."

Along with the extermination of the Indian went the extermination of the buffalo. Between 1872 and 1874, over one and a half million buffalo were killed, many by buffalo hunters hired by the railroad, many others by white sportsmen and women. Several of the railroads advertised the possibility of shooting a buffalo from the comfort of your coach seat. William Blackmore, traveling on the north bank of the Arkansas River in the spring of 1873, wrote that "there was a continual line of putrescent carcasses so that the air was rendered pestilential and offensive to the last degree." Travelers on the Kansas Pacific Railroad were advised to wrap bandanas around their faces to mask the smell of the rotting animals that lined the tracks.

Sherman, Sheridan and other Army leaders had taken

the position that the quickest way to tame the roving natives was to hurry along the extermination of the buffalo. These men believed that in a world without buffalo, there might be red men on the earth, but they would not be Indians.

In many ways parallel to the late-nineteenth-century European settlers' attempted eradication of the Indian and the buffalo is the late twentieth-century Americans' attempted eradication of the wolf. In Wyoming, attitudes toward wolf reintroduction and protection are a pretty good measure of other social attitudes a person holds. The Lakota writer Joe Marshall maintains that the wolf is simply the twentieth century stand-in for the Plains Indian. Marshall holds that the wolf is, along with the Indian, one of the continent's first peoples and that those who wish to eradicate the wolf are acting out their unspoken continuing desire to kill Indians.

Then there is the Wyoming Toad (bufo hemiophrys Baxteri), an animal whose sole habitat is in one small area of southeastern Wyoming. Since "discovering" this toad, biologists have watched its population steadily decline. No amount of protection or study seems to reverse this pattern. The toad's ultimate disappearance seems a logical outgrowth of our land use practices—of habitat destruction.

The clearing out of the Indians and of the buffalo was deliberate. But the destruction of this other species is an "accident," an outgrowth of the relationship between some human beings and the rest of the world. No one now means to eradicate the Wyoming Toad just as no one in the last century meant to eradicate the passenger pigeon. This accidental extermination is more frightening and ominous to me for it means we are even less likely to change the behavior that leads to the death of the other.

Now I must backtrack to Jean and John Esponda and those early days. In the midst of the struggle to exterminate the Indian and the buffalo, as though fully aware of how things would end, the great cattlemen had founded their vast ranches. Without title to the land, they had exploited the open range. Their power was based on two pillars—the custom of allowing stock owners to graze their animals at will, and simple force—the hired gunman and money.

In the cattlemen's view, cows would replace the buffalo, corn and wheat would replace the local grasses, and white people would replace the Indians.

In 1892, members of the Wyoming Stock Growers Association, the political voice of the large cattlemen, angered by what they took to be criminal intrusions on their way of life, hired twenty-seven gunmen (twenty-five of them Texans) and with twenty-one of their own members, three teamsters, a surgeon and two newspaper reporters invaded Johnson County. That was only ten years before the Espondas' arrival in Wyoming, yet the brothers knew nothing of the invasion.

The stock growers had compiled a list of seventy men who were to be "eliminated" for their "crimes." These crimes were largely "rustling." But the root of the conflict was based on the recent influx of settlers who were filing land claims under the U.S. Homestead Act. Often the claims were filed along creeks and rivers. The new settlers planned to farm, or to ranch on a small scale. They fenced their land, keeping the large cattlemen's stock away from water.

Wyoming stock law only made matters worse. Mavericks—unbranded calves—were by law to be gathered in the large yearly roundups. At these roundups, maverick calves would be branded in proportion to the cattle each rancher owned. The divvying up of stock was hampered by the fact that only certain owners were allowed to participate in the roundups. Large owners. The small ranchers complained bitterly that their unbranded stock was being stolen by large owners at the roundups.

Reform of the maverick laws was hampered by the fact that Wyoming statute made the Wyoming Stock Growers Association the policing agency for stock laws. This is analogous to the old saying about making the fox the guardian of the henhouse.

Out of touch with northern Wyoming's newcomers—the homestead farmers and small ranchers—the large stockmen felt their invasion of Johnson County would trigger a popular uprising in their favor. After taking the train north from Cheyenne to Casper, and then going by wagon and horseback farther north, the invaders laid siege to a small ranch building in southern Johnson County and there murdered two men— Nate Champion and Nick Ray. Instead of galvanizing local opinion in their favor, these murders caused a violent outburst of resentment. The invaders found themselves surrounded by several hundred deputized Johnson County residents howling for the blood of the rich and powerful.

Through the intervention of Wyoming's governor Amos Barber, its senators Francis E. Warren and Joseph M. Carey, and President Benjamin Harrison, the murderers were taken into custody by the U.S. Army and removed three hundred miles to the south. A hotel was converted to a makeshift jail. Food and linen services were arranged. Johnson County was billed for the upkeep of the fifty prisoners. But Johnson County couldn't afford to pay. The Texans were released on bond and returned home. The Wyoming residents smoked and chatted until their release. No one was convicted for the murders. No one was tried.

Another group of cattlemen, annoyed by the encroachment of small homesteaders in the Sweetwater valley, took it upon themselves to hang Jim Averell and Ella Watson. Averell had made himself a nuisance by repeatedly writing letters to the editor of the Casper Weekly Mail condemning the large "range hogs." And Ella Watson was beginning to build up a little herd of cattle of her own. Ella Watson and Jim Averell were kidnapped and hanged by upstanding gentlemen of the community. Watson died the only woman lynched in Wyoming's history. Again, the murderers were never tried.

In the Rock Springs coal mines, white workers, tired of what they perceived to be favoritism shown to Chinese miners by the mine owners, left their underground coal rooms and poured out into the sunlight. They ran through Rock Springs' Chinatown, a city of shacks made from cardboard and tin tied together with dust. They swung clubs and wielded knives and guns. They set fire to everything that would burn, including human beings. Twenty-eight Chinese people were murdered. The blood was left where it lay and no one was tried for the murders.

On the west side of the Bighorn Mountains two sheepherders were murdered. The murderers also killed the herders' dogs and ten thousand sheep. I can't imagine the technique that was used to kill ten thousand sheep and the historical record is mute on this point. Having finished with the sheep, the murderers then burned the herders' wagons.

In southern Wyoming shortly before the Espondas'

arrival in the state, Tom Horn, a Stock Growers Association range detective—a euphemism for hired gun—mistakenly killed a fourteen-year-old boy who was wearing his father's coat and hat. Horn, as fall guy and symbol of changing times, was hanged. To this day, his guilt or innocence is hotly debated.

Jean and John Esponda stood shading their eyes against the sun, or, had they known, against all that blood. Either way, it was a grim picture that came to them. "I don't know," Jean said, and decided to try his luck elsewhere. He left northern Wyoming and never returned. But Jean's brother John continued to see potential in Johnson County.

"Wyoming land not much good, no grass, no water for sheep," John Esponda is reported to have written home to Baigorry. "But open, plenty of space for a man to get a start. I make do."

John Esponda turned in a full circle, surveying the land to the north, east, south and west. The smile on his face was an ironic one, but it had nothing to do with the fact that his brother had brought him to Wyoming then left. Neither was it that he appeared to be a successor to murderers and charlatans. As I've said, of this he knew nothing. The irony was in coming here to work the land. The land really did look terrible to him. The grass was sparse and mostly brown and hard. Sheep would wear out their mouths on that in four or five years.

Wyoming wasn't much like the rain-shrouded Pyrenees or like California. The only liquid was all that blood. By 1902, though, the blood had dried into the earth and the lynchings, invasions and murders by hire were becoming myth and legend. The land might look unproductive, but it was land, open and waiting.

John Esponda had said he would make do. Throughout history no matter where the Basques have landed, they have made do. The Basque people—the Euskaldunak—are believed to be the first human residents of Europe. Some scholars believe the Basques are the direct descendants of Cro-Magnon man. Others say the Basques are immigrants, having settled in the Pyrenees Mountains and along the shores of the Bay of Biscay perhaps seventy-five thousand years ago. Still others put the Basque arrival between twenty-five and fifty thousand years ago, and a last group of historians believe the Basques moved into the Pyrenees region as recently as the year 3000 B.C.E. If this recent date is accurate, then the Basques absorbed the people already living in the area.

Scholars are careful, unwilling to commit themselves and then be found in error. So all that can be said with certainty is that the Basques live in the Pyrenees and have for a long time.

Whatever dates we use, the Basques were settled in the Pyrenees long before the Roman Legions entered the Iberian Peninsula around 200 B.C.E. to conquer the declining Carthaginians. The first written records concerning the Basques are by Roman writers. The Romans noted that the Basques were operating ironworks. These Basques were the most industrialized people of their time.

The Basques might have come from the north of India, or they might have come from Turkey. Genetic studies have often been used to show that the Basques are unrelated to other European peoples. Basques have the highest rate of blood type O and the lowest rate of blood type B in Europe. They have the highest rate of the Rh negative factor of any population in the world.

These genetic markers are not as important in determining Basqueness as is language. Basques speak Basque—Euskara. This tongue is not a member of the Romance family of languages. In sound and structure it bears little resemblance to the two most widely known Latin-based languages—French and Spanish—spoken in the Basque region. In fact, Euskara seems to be only distantly related to any other European language.

The Basques contend theirs is the original language given by God to mankind in the Garden of Eden, Eden having been in the Basque Country. This means that the Basques were the people who committed the first act of disobedience. It also means that when the Basques left the Garden, they forgot the Lord and wandered as pagans for some unknown number of thousands of years. When they returned they lived for perhaps seventy-five thousand years more before they recognized the Lord amongst them again.

Euskara is the tongue that was spoken by all human beings before the Tower of Babel. Euskara is not only the language given by God to humanity, but is God's own language, so difficult to learn that even Basque children struggle to imitate their parents' words, and outsiders are rarely encouraged in their attempts to speak.

An older Basque woman once told me the only way I would learn the language would be to marry a Basque girl and live with her for at least seven years. "Remember," she said, "the days they do not matter, but the nights, there is where you will learn."

The Euskaldunak are often called the "Mystery People of Europe," though this may be little more than a public relations ploy executed by the Basques themselves to throw outsiders off the track.

John Esponda wrote home to Baigorry explaining that there was plenty of land in northern Wyoming, that a man could take his wages as a herder in sheep, graze those sheep with the owner's until he had a band of his own and finally move off onto open land to start his own ranch. That story quickly brought other Basques from the Pyrenees to the Bighorns.

Thanks to Jean Esponda's chance encounter and his brother John's vision, these Basques found themselves, perhaps for the second time, in a land without an ocean. As John was, they were painfully aware of the arid emptiness of Wyoming, but no matter how foreign Wyoming was, it offered the immigrant the possibility of becoming a landowner. This meant a great deal to people who had for centuries lived in a small, crowded, poor land.

Following his brother, John Esponda knew that he would stay in America. After he arrived in Wyoming, he had a small revelation—work, make do, perhaps something better than you expect will happen.

The Basques who came to Johnson County between 1902 and 1920 almost all became prominent ranchers in the sheep boom of the first two decades of the twentieth century. John Esponda was perhaps the most prominent and successful of them all. Something much better than he had expected had happened. For the rest of his life, he remained surprised by this.

♦

The next round of Basque immigrants to northern Wyoming included my wife's paternal grandmother Jeanne Etchemendy Iberlin who came from near the village of Arneguy.

At age fourteen, working away from home as a maid in St. Jean-Pied-de-Port, Jeanne Etchemendy dreamed of going to Tunisia or America. In late 1920, at the age of twenty-nine, she arrived in Buffalo with nothing more than the promise of work and the presence of other Basque people. In Buffalo, she worked as hard as she had in St. Jean. But Buffalo was even farther from home. The Basque herders were almost never in town. Her employers were English-speaking non-Basques. Now Jeanne dreamed of earning enough money to return to the Basque homeland and start her own business—a butcher shop.

The possibilities for her didn't seem as grand as they had seemed for John Esponda when he arrived eighteen years earlier.

Working hard all day and sitting alone at night, Jeanne asked herself what she had come to. She knew work as well as any of the Basques in Wyoming and did not complain when presented with hard work. But what of the rest of life? The shuffle and leap of the fandango and the arin-arin, the shouts that accompany the dancing, the intense focus of the players and watchers at the Saturday jai-alai matches, the Sunday walks in the sweet sun, the cool light bouncing from the leaves of the trees, the picnics with friends, the young people rolling down deep greeny soft hillsides.

She felt only loss. Jeanne knew she had to accept loss in order to have gain. Sometimes it seemed to her that she faced a life of nothing—forty, fifty, sixty years, perhaps, of nothing stretching out ahead of her. Those were her moments of loneliness and despair. But they passed. As sure as the snow fell again and bathed the empty land of Wyoming in brilliance and beauty, as sure as that, there was going to be something for Jeanne.

In those early months as a hired worker, Jeanne walked twice a day from her house in town to a pasture a mile away. There in an uninsulated unheated shed made from rough-cut planks she milked her cow. Twice a day, no matter the season, no matter her exhaustion. Letting her hands rise from her pockets she warmed them under her arms, she blew across her fingertips. Firmly, she squeezed and pulled, sliding the inside of her thumb and palm along the cow's pink shining skin. She turned the cow's udder so that the snow-white milk struck the pail obliquely, the way rain strikes a windowpane and slides without splashing. She thought about rain falling and about the beauty of snow.

The bucket full, Jeanne hefted it up and walked home. She followed the same route each day and each day she saw a little more how her new town, Buffalo, Wyoming—it sounded strange to shape the syllables in her mouth—was not so different from the Basque homeland. Everywhere in the world is more like everywhere else than she would have thought.

"Seems like maybe I had that thought some other day," Jeanne whispered to herself. And smiled. "Well, it's hard to think up new thoughts when you're worn out. It's true that work gives a person a sense of place, but it's also true," she laughed, "that work gets me tired."

With that laugh, Jeanne Etchemendy had the same feeling of revelation that John Esponda had experienced earlier. Like every Basque person I've known, she put her faith in the dignity of work. She would work hard, make do, and perhaps something good would happen.

In Buffalo Jeanne Etchemendy was a young single

Basque woman among forty solitary Basque sheepherders, each herder working to start his own ranch and his own family. In August of 1921, less than a year after arriving in Wyoming, Jeanne married John Iberlin who came from near the village of Banca, the house of Gattulinea. Basque people have always been known more by the house they come from than by their family name. The house name Gattulinea is from the word Gatilu—the cup. Now John and Jeanne's cup was being filled.

For their honeymoon, the newlyweds drove with John Esponda to Yellowstone Park. It was Esponda's car. There is a picture of them all during the honeymoon. John Esponda stands off to one side of the frame staring at something we can't see. His large moustache doesn't quite hide the Esponda grin he shared with his older brother Jean. The newlyweds stand in front of the car staring directly into the camera. Jeanne is wearing a white hat and a dark suit brought from Europe. Her face is wide and smooth. Her left hand rests on her hip and her elbow just nudges her new husband's arm. She neither smiles nor frowns, as if presenting to the camera a mask of neutrality.

Years later, as she sat up one night, making over her husband's worn wool shirts for her two sons Simon and Johnny, she suddenly laughed out loud. The three men, engrossed in discussing the next day's work, looked at her but said nothing. They didn't ask, "What's so funny?" Or "Are you alright?" Jeanne kept sewing, sitting up waiting on the nights when John, Simon and Johnny were out late working, during lambing and shearing.

It seemed she needed almost no sleep. She was a woman awakened by her chores, by her task, by her life. The years passed but it seemed she would live forever. And whether it was in the cabin at the ranch or in the house in town, the work was always waiting—the chickens in the yard, the pig in its pen. Each year the time came to kill the pig, to make cured pork, make lard, make sausages, make ham. And each year the time came to preserve vegetables—to can the beans, carrots, cabbage, tomatoes, all the wealth Jeanne had coaxed from the reluctant earth.

Not to mention sheep—moving sheep, doctoring sick sheep, shearing sheep, docking sheep, branding sheep. The work that was mostly the men's but which she helped with, too. The bad years and the good. There was the especially bad year when of five thousand sheep the bank took the best three thousand to cover the mortgage payment.

It was almost a relief. The idea of surrender flickered in Jeanne's mind. Flickered and passed. No quitting now—there were two thousand broken-mouthed ewes with which to begin again. So with husband John, and her children Simon, Johnny and now Madeleine and Mary Louise, Jeanne began again.

As John Esponda had done years earlier, Jeanne Etchemendy Iberlin did now. She looked around her, turning from north to east to south to west. She felt the wind against her wide face. The wind blew from this direction then from that. For much of the year the temperature was too cold, then suddenly it was too hot and just when a little breeze would be a relief, the wind stopped.

I think it sometimes must have seemed crazy to find such a life worth it, but Jeanne did. "Hard, shmard," she said, laughing as she imitated English slang she'd heard on the radio. Throughout her life, she joked about the English language which somehow represented hardship. At age ninety-seven, after sixty-eight years in Wyoming, Jeanne suffered a stroke. She recovered fully except that she could no longer speak English. Only Basque words came from her mouth.

In many ways the second-round immigrant Jeanne Etchemendy's life had been as successful as first-round immigrant John Esponda's. She, too, ended as part of a successful Wyoming sheep ranching family. Still, the work she did to make her success seems more obvious, more demanding, more unremitting. And in the end, her loss of the English language five years before her death at the age of 102 serves as a reminder that she would always be standing at the gate looking in.

The Basque people admire physical strength. They admire, too, the willingness to face deprivation in pursuit of a goal. For me, John Esponda and Jeanne Etchemendy Iberlin represent perfectly these admirable traits.

As I come closer to the present, closer to people amongst whom I live, whose lapses and complaints I must respect, my own judgment concerning others becomes murkier, more confusing.

♦

Lucien Laurent Millox was one of the Basque immigrants who came after both John Esponda and Jeanne Etchemendy Iberlin. Born in Bayonne, France, Lucien attended school there in a convent. After World War Two, he served in the French Foreign Legion and then came to the United States, to Johnson County, Wyoming, where, though he found other Basques, he didn't exactly find a home. Always slightly distant from his American surroundings,

Lucien was a reminder of the tension of the Basque immigrant's life—perched or maybe one could say poised between two worlds, not quite having left one behind and not quite having entered the other.

By the time Lucien arrived in Wyoming, there was little land left to be bought. Fencing had become increasingly common so that fewer herders were needed. Lucien worked all of his life for other ranchers, mostly fellow Basques. He never owned a ranch of his own.

From his first days in Powder River country, he was known to have a sheepwagon that sparkled. He kept everything in it immaculately clean, including the tea towels with which he dried his few dishes.

Lucien was a strong, stoutly built man. He had a low forehead and a round face with widely set eyes. His nostrils flared below high cheekbones and above a large chin. His hair was dark and curly. Though he was not handsome, he might, with a little more material success, have pleased many a prospective bride.

Sometimes after a week of work, Lucien would go to town to the bar. After three or four drinks, he would challenge his drinking companion to a fight. The usual response to such a challenge was "Lucien, let's not fight tonight. Let's fight tomorrow at twelve o'clock."

And Lucien would say, "That's a good idea. We'll fight tomorrow at twelve." So there would be no fight. Lucien would pull out a wad of bills—most likely all the money he had—and, waving the money around the room, would suggest that someone go in with him to buy a ranch. When no one took him up on this, Lucien would offer to help some other landless Basque buy himself his own ranch.

Lucien, who might seem to outsiders a clown, or simply a failure, has become for me a symbol of Basque hopes and fears. He worked as hard as anyone and yet he somehow never quite made it in American society. He had come to the United States after the boom years between 1900 and 1920. Even the arid land to the east of the mountains was mostly claimed. Had he found a piece of land to buy, prices were high and his wages covered little more than the cost of getting by from year to year. At the rate at which he could save, he'd have to live longer than Jeanne Iberlin in order to have enough money for a down payment.

It seemed hopeless and he spent his money on momentary pleasure. He was moody and generous, making periodic grand gestures toward his fellows. He served as a reminder to people that getting ahead required at least a little selfishness. Too much generosity led nowhere.

One summer night in 1989, after sixty-three years on this earth, Lucien found himself once again in the bar nursing beer after beer. There he was, standing firmly at the border dividing hard worker from old age. He had been joking and playing—waving his wad of money around, making mock threats and silly offers. His only hope now was that for every joke he made, he gained another inch of the grazing land of Heaven.

Finally, as it grew later and quieter, Lucien asked a stranger for a ride home. The stranger obliged and the two men got up to leave. This is the second to the last thing anyone knows for certain about Lucien's life.

The last thing we know is that Lucien was murdered. The police report states that he was beaten to death with a blunt instrument—perhaps a shovel or other hand tool—and that his body was found at the side of the road under the Rock Creek overpass of Interstate 90 north of Buffalo.

No one knows why Lucien was murdered. No one who'd been at the bar could remember seeing him get into the pickup, nor if there'd been a pickup with out-of-state plates parked on the street in front of the bar. People laughed ruefully when the sheriff asked if anyone remembered the plate number on the pickup.

"Lucien just asked the man for a ride home," an older Basque said. "There was nothing strange about the guy. He sat at the bar, had a few drinks, not too many, talked some, listened some. When he got ready to leave, Lucien asked him for a ride. There's always somebody comes in from out of town on a Saturday. Some guy passing through."

The next morning a local rancher going into town saw a large pool of blood on the road at the Rock Creek overpass. "I wondered what kind of animal could have left so much blood on the road," he later told the sheriff. "But I didn't see any sign of anything. There were no skid marks, nothing. You know, if you hit a big raccoon and drive over it, you drag it and it makes a mess, you know what I mean. There's bits of fur and blood and the entrails dragged along the asphalt. Excuse me, but that's how it is. Well, there was nothing but blood. So when I come back from town I stopped to see what had happened."

Concerning the life and death of Lucien Laurent Millox, here is where our knowledge begins again. It was Lucien's blood that lay on the road. Lucien was dead and even if he were only almost dead and able to groan and call out for help, there would still be the distance between houses and the fact of his face being smashed, his bloody blackened eyes swollen shut.

I wonder if it was sometime during that night that Lucien allowed himself the bitterness to think that he too had lived his life by the same motto that John Esponda and Jeanne Etchemendy Iberlin had lived by: "Work, make do, perhaps something better than you expect will happen." Things hadn't worked out for Lucien the way they had for those earlier Basques.

Six men picked up Lucien's body and carried it to the Holy Church where the priest told the brief story of Lucien's life. "He was as important as Gorbachev," the priest said. And more to the point, "He was as important as the Pope." That made everyone think for a moment—"as important as the Pope."

After Mass, the battered body was once again picked up and carried away for burial. Domingo Martirena, Mike Iriberry, Charles Marton, Orturo Vasco, John Esponda, Jr. and Mitch Esponda lifted Lucien to their shoulders and began to walk. They walked carefully, balancing the heavy box so that it moved smoothly through space. They carried Lucien away.

After Lucien's funeral, my three-year-old nephew Matthew Spotted Calf Iberlin, the child of a Basque mother and a Lakota father, came home with me. While John, Jeanne and Lucien represent the changing experience of three waves of Basque immigrants to northern Wyoming, Matthew and I each represent something completely different.

Matthew was born in this country; he is of mixed heritage. His expectations of America will be tempered not only by the increasing difficulties the Basque immigrants faced, but by the historical knowledge of his Lakota people.

Matthew and I changed out of our funeral clothes and

went outside to work in the yard. I began pulling dandelions from the lawn.

"Why do you pull these flowers out?" Matthew asked.

"I don't want them here," I said, "They're weeds, stronger than the grass. If I don't dig them out, they'll spread and take over. Soon there'll be no grass."

I was pulling the dandelions out with a long steel tool that had a sharp forked end. Matthew wanted to help. He asked for the tool and I handed it to him. He shoved the slender blade of steel into the ground and struggled to pull up the plant. Mostly he only got the flower while the root remained firmly planted, deep in the earth. Matthew worked away. He was silent; he expressed neither disappointment nor hope. He simply tried to pull out the dandelions. Then he spoke again. "How do you say weed in Basque?"

"I don't know." I said.

Wyoming is neither Arneguy nor Baigorry. I'm Matthew's uncle but only by marriage. I'm not Basque and I don't know the word.

"I don't know, Matthew." I said again, "We'll have to ask your grandfather Atatchi Simon."

My nephew Matthew Spotted Calf Iberlin isn't a Basque boy. He isn't a Lakota boy. Buried in his history are other people that he isn't—German–Russians, for one. And Matthew isn't an American either. One could turn all these "isn'ts" around and say Matthew is all these things—he is Basque, Lakota, German–Russian, American.

Watching Matthew work, I thought not only about his life but also about Lucien and about John Esponda and Jeanne Etchemendy Iberlin. I thought about myself.

Each of us came to Wyoming a stranger. When I arrived

thirteen years ago, I couldn't imagine staying, but, like the Basques, I have. I've married into a Basque ranching family. Because I don't live on the ranch, I'm usually only there to work.

Now and again, though, without a job to do, my wife Margo, daughter Caitlin, mother in-law Dollie and I spend a night together at the ranch. I remember a particular night when we slept outside with the stars' milky light shining on our faces. Next to where we laid out our sleeping bags, on a flat above the Four Mile Creek bed, we set up two tents just in case we got a thunderstorm or late snow. Both were more a hope than a fear. We were longing for water.

The creek, as usual, was dry. The air, hot and windy all day, was cold and windy. We lit a tiny low fire in the middle of the creek bed. Surrounded by tinder-dry cottonwoods, such a fire was dangerous but we lit it anyway. Lifted by the wind, sparks flashed and leapt down the dusty wash. It was a miniature fireworks show held under imaginary water, a wavering shining faraway brilliance. We stood close to it trying to contain the magic. Really, trying to keep the sparks out of the cottonwoods.

We talked about the day. Caitlin was three then and crazy about photography. She had spent the afternoon walking around taking pictures—lichen on a rock, a dead cottonwood branch, the back of Dollie's head, a mudhole in a cutbank, a piece of mica, a frightened lizard, the sky. Caitlin was born in Buffalo, as were her mother Margo and grandmother Dollie.

In the Bible it says "you are dust, and to dust you shall return." I felt that Dollie, Margo and Caitlin were of this earth. I, on the other hand, seemed to have arrived from

Mars and only now was coming in for a landing, finding my way home. In this way, perhaps I'm more like the early Basque immigrants than I am like my American born Basque family.

Each of us who has come to Wyoming from elsewhere comes eventually to the same moment. John Esponda experienced that moment when, following his brother, he stepped down off the train in Buffalo in 1902. Jeanne Etchemendy Iberlin experienced it as she sat sewing after supper in 1934 and felt a smile cross her face. Lucien Laurent Millox experienced it as his assailant approached him late one night in 1989. This moment is one of self-knowledge. It can come by force of insight or press of circumstance.

All of us who have come to Wyoming from elsewhere find ourselves surrounded by a world of sky and space and sage. We stand with one hand shading our eyes so as to be able to see and with the other hand carrying our suitcases, the baggage of everything we were before we arrived here.

The Basques of Buffalo came mostly from Arneguy, but also from Baigorry, Banca, Lasse, Irissarry, Anheaux, Esterencuby, Osses, Ahaxe, Irouleguy, Ondarrole, Ascarat and Ihaldy in the northern Basque Country; and from Valcarlos, Oyantzun, Zumbilla and Sabilla in the southern Basque Country.

I want to name some of the people who came from those places to make this place for me. I want to remember them and to remind others of their presence among us: John and Martin Camino, Jean and Santiago Curutchet, Dominica, Pete, Jeanne, Catherine, Marie and Bernard Etchemendy, Dominica Etcheverry, Jeanne Ansolabehere, John Esponda, Peter Bordarrampe, Catherine, Grace and Marie Iriart,

Domingo Martirena, Martin Falxa, Simon and Marie
Harriet, John Iberlin, Gaston Irigaray, Bernard Marton,
Santiago and Sebastian Michelena, Peter and Marie
Urrizaga, Martin Urruty, Fermin Reculusa, Mitchell and
Pierre Iriberry, Jean Indart, Antoine Cubialde, Celestina
Arrechea, Peter Faure, Gaston Irigaray, Marie Elizalde,
Sauveur Inchauspe, Domingo Goyhenex, Arnaud Ausqui.

Each of these Basques came at the urging of another—a
friend, a sister, a brother, an uncle, a fellow villager. It was
somehow as it had been in the Bible, one Basque brought
forth a second, and soon the land surrounding Buffalo,
Wyoming, was another province—albeit distant—of the
Basque homeland.

Economy ♦

The work I do at Four Mile Ranch—both the windmill maintenance and everything else—is useful work, fulfilling. Doing it I feel alive. I am inside a universe, not outside looking in. But when asked about my profession, I tell people I'm a poet or, sometimes, I say writer, but never rancher.

A poet friend of mine was telling me about his experience of traveling on airplanes. "You ever notice," he asked, "that mostly people on planes don't talk to each other? Except when the food comes. Then they start talking. Like it's impolite, even unthinkable to eat in silence. It's like eating has to happen as part of a social scene."

"I've noticed that," I say.

"So the food comes," my friend goes on, "and people start in with the 'What do you do?' If I want to talk, I tell them I'm a writer. That gets 'em going. Nearly everyone in America is a writer and is longing to talk about it. But sometimes I don't want to talk to a stranger. If that's how I'm feeling when the person asks me what I do, I say I'm a poet. A deathly hush comes over the trays and I'm left completely to my own resources. Ha! No one wants to talk to a poet."

I don't make much money writing so maybe I shouldn't say that it's my profession—poet or otherwise. On the other hand, I make no money working on the ranch. Still, it's my work and ranchers have never made much money. Even today there are ranchers who have chosen their profession knowing there's no money in it, or not thinking about money, not caring. There are ranchers who would stay on their places even if they had to get other jobs in town in order to be able to ranch. If the federal government passed a law saying you had to pay thousands of dollars a year for the right to ranch, a lot of ranchers would do it. They'd clerk in stores, teach school, work at the post office, sell real estate, be nurses, bank tellers, insurance agents—anything in order to earn the money to pay for the right to ranch.

Now that I think of it, that's just about exactly what it takes for both ranchers and poets to keep at their work. It's something they have in common—this unusual relationship to the economy.

Henry David Thoreau once boasted that his was one of the finest libraries in Concord—a thousand volumes, seven hundred and fifty of which he had written himself. Recently, I learned that a new book by Thoreau has been published. Over one hundred years after his death, someone is still earning money from his words, though it isn't Thoreau. This is often the way our economy works.

One fall the oil company was looking to drill a well in the Bridge Pasture at Four Mile. The company geologists pored over the maps—not to pick the best spot but to pick the best spot on land where the subsurface rights had been leased by the federal government to the oil company. They hoped to avoid paying mineral royalties to Simon by not drilling on any land where he retained the subsurface rights.

When early homesteaders received the deed to their land, they were granted ownership of both surface and subsurface rights. Fairly quickly it became clear that there were things of value beneath the surface—oil, gas, coal, uranium. Homestead law was then rewritten so that the homesteader's property rights were granted only for the surface. The federal government held in perpetuity all subsurface rights, which it could lease out. This means that today in areas which were originally homestead land, there is often a byzantine checkerboard of rights underground. That checkerboard rarely matches the equally byzantine checkerboard of ownership above ground.

"How much it cost to drill a hole for me for a water well?" Simon asked the oil company drillers.

"Case of whisky and we'll put a hole down for you." the crew boss said.

"You got it," Simon said, and so there's another hole down to water in the Bridge Pasture. There isn't actually a windmill there though. Simon wants to put in an electric mill. "More efficient and there's power close enough to run lines without it costing an arm and a leg," he says.

I don't fully agree. "Seems like electric mills just end up getting hit by lightning and quit working," I argue. "The submersible pumps are expensive and you can't really fix them. When they break you gotta buy a new one. No matter what they tell you about corrosion-resistant materials, like as not the wiring's gonna corrode underwater." I don't tell Simon the rest—that I hate the parade of power poles for miles across the Breaks just to bring power to one electric motor in the middle of nowhere. Sky full of wires.

"Way less ongoing maintenance with an electric mill," Simon reminds me.

"Maybe," I hedge. "But at least you can fix a windmill on your own and remember, there's no mill here yet and out at the edge of this pasture there's a mill bringing up water every time the wind blows."

"Wanta bet?" Simon says. We take the pickup over the ridge to the Bridge West mill. The wind's blowing but the fan's not moving.

"Shit," I say.

Simon chuckles. Then when we get there, he jumps out, releases the brake on the mill and shouts "April Fool!" I kick the ground and raise a little dust. In a few minutes water begins to pour out of the pipe. "Come on, David," Simon says. "We'll keep the old mills going, let's just try the electric ones too, huh?"

And so, keeping in mind the economy, we have.

At our house in town, I grow a garden in which are planted many foods. One is cilantro, a tangy leafy green the flavor of which one friend likens to soap. "How can you eat that stuff?" she asks.

But, to me, cilantro is wonderful. This food that I find to be delicious tastes like soap to my friend. To paraphrase Shakespeare, if you open my throat, do you not find taste buds? Yes, but they are not the same as yours. Shakespeare felt compelled to show that we are all the same and so should be treated with dignity and respect. We are not the same. We suffer and cherish great differences amongst one another. Jesus did not call us to love our friends. "Love your enemy," he said. And the Dalai Lama reminds us that our enemy is our teacher.

The economy's big problem is that it assumes we all have the same taste buds. The economy wants us to swear unswerving sameness before it will love us. We can tell the economy to screw off, loving each other in spite of and because of our differences.

Along with cilantro, I grow tomatoes, corn, beans, edible pod peas, carrots, spinach, several kinds of lettuce, raspberries, strawberries, acorn squash, pumpkin, and, in some years, eggplant. In a separate, smaller spot I grow many varieties of pepper including bell, jalapeño, Anaheim, Hungarian hot, and cherry. Below the raspberries I keep a long bed for two varieties of mint. I consider mint to be an integral part of a well developed subsistence agriculture program.

My daughter swings in the hammock above the mint bed. As she drifts by she lets her arm hang over the edge and plucks off a mint leaf which she chews for the bright tangy flavor. When she's chewed the mint into a gooey pulp, she spits it out. She says the darker leaves taste better than the lighter ones. I make iced mint water. In the fall, I dry some mint and on cold winter nights make hot mint tea.

Each year I also plant cantaloupe, not so much for the rich orange fruit which rarely ripens in our climate but because I have hope. In one year of the past ten, cantaloupe has come to fruition. Nothing has tasted so delicious.

Our average frost-free growing season is 98 days. That doesn't tell us much about gardening though since the average is based on yearly fluctuations of from 48 to 175 frost-free days. The 48 end is the more usual. When I despair of the possibility of growing the food I need in order to keep myself and my family alive, I think of my friends in Jackson in the far west of Wyoming. Their growing season is as short as 35 days, and 50 or 60 frost-free days are a great many indeed. But Jackson's is another economy, utterly unlike that of my part of the state.

That statement is not quite true. Jackson's economy is different from the rest of Wyoming's not so much in kind as in scale. The east face of the Bighorn Range is the area where, as a friend of mine jokes, "the peaceful range wars ended." Nearly the entire cowboy Hollywood mythology of the arid interior West is based on a few events that took place in the Bighorn Mountains and in the Powder River Basin to the east of these mountains—the Wagon Box Fight, the Fetterman Massacre, the Johnson County Invasion, Hole in the Wall and, slightly to the north, the Little Big Horn.

These events have become the basis for a pan-Western popular history. And this popular history, along with the "grandeur of the scenery," is increasingly becoming the basis for a tourism-based economy in Wyoming—all of Wyoming. Places that were not so long ago thought by many to be barren, desolate, harsh, too cold, too hot, and culturally backward are now considered charming and romantic. That's where the contemporary Wyoming economy comes in.

The Jackson Chamber of Commerce puts out a brochure meant to entice visitors and their money to the town. One of the attractions listed in the brochure is the reenactment each Saturday evening of "an old-fashioned Western gunfight on the square."

I have tried to picture this scenario changed from the Old West to Vietnam. I imagine a small town in the Mekong

Delta of Vietnam advertising the reenactment of "an old fashioned fire fight *sur la place centrale.*" I guess it would be complete with malaria and cholera, with hunger, napalm, Russian-made rocket launchers and distant B-52 bombers raining death from the stratosphere. At the end everyone would dive for the tunnels, hugging the damp earth. For the Americans it would be incoming, sappers, fragging, Huey helicopters, medevac.

Just as Jackson's economy differs from ours in Buffalo only in scale, so do the two gunfights I've mentioned differ only in scale. The very few times when two men faced each other with guns on a street in some frozen or dusty or muddy Wyoming town, one of them often ended up dead. For the dead man there was no romance in the gunfight. And, sadly, there is nothing old-fashioned about gunfights.

It's true that the gun played a large role in the settling of Wyoming, and that the gun's legacy is with us today. In the nineteenth century, we had several types of gunfighters including both the bad hombres and the Robin Hood type train robbers. We also had the town sheriffs, Pinkerton detectives, Stock Growers Association inspectors, United States marshals, soldiers and scouts—both Indian and white—and buffalo hunters hired to clear the prairies. In addition to all of these, there was the generic cowboy, merely a hobbyist when it came to guns.

We're standing in the Jackson town square with our cameras ready. There are two cowboys with their six-shooters strapped to their thighs. They step off the wooden sidewalk and into the dusty street. The merciless sun pounds down on their broad brimmed hats. There is a steely glint in each man's eyes. Young boys peek out from behind the corners of the buildings, anxious to see the battle. The two men stand motionless.

In the old days, the air was so still that the buzzing of flies thundered in the ears of the entire town. The air remains still but now we hear the buzzing of camcorders as the old-fashioned gunfight is about to begin.

After what seems an eternity, the men draw. But what's this? What if at the end of the guns' pearl handles there were no gun barrels? What if, instead, each man drew from his holster a rigid slightly crooked penis? Finally, a proper symbol of the struggle now being played out in Wyoming, the struggle to prove that one is an authentic resident of the real West—more manly and more Western than thou.

I'll assume the two cowboys are still standing there. How can they shoot straight with those crooked penises? Both the tourists and the locals are shocked. They just came for a simple reenactment of an old-time gunfight. Some people put away their cameras as fast as they can. Others begin furiously recording the scene.

Finally, the gunfighters pull their triggers and out fly two creamy plugs of semen. Splot! Each man is hit in the face by the other's ejaculation. The range wars may have ended but the semen is still on our faces and hands. What are we going to do with an economy like this?

In Wyoming in the 1990s the main thing is to figure out how to make a living. It's hard what with all the squabbling in the dusty street, those messy gunfighters out there.

One story told here is that the region was settled by rugged individualists—mostly men and mostly white—who acted alone. These men are said to have made the West. Though the lives of my ranching neighbors teach that those who act alone don't survive, romance clings to the rugged individualist model.

Related to our idea that it was the lone individual who built the West is our belief in action. In *Riding the White Horse Home,* Teresa Jordan tells the story of her family and its ranch in the southeastern part of Wyoming. Teresa speaks of the admiration she felt as a child for the men who worked on the ranch—men who could do things. I too admire the ability to do things—to fix fence, brand sheep or cows, work sixteen hours a day calving or shearing and docking, build a barn, make and repair your own tools. These are the things men have traditionally done. Then there's the work that's mostly been done by women. Teresa and I both admire this work, too. It is still the ability to do things—bake bread, can tomatoes, cultivate a flower garden, sing to a child, write a letter, console a friend. There are so many things that we can do. Let's do them.

But sometimes I wonder. The lake freezes in winter and becomes silent and still. The fish who live in the lake survive by doing less. They grow quiet and patient. Each spring they awaken to a planet reborn. We can learn from these fish the something that is very little, even nothing.

Many Wyoming citizens believe that we need more people, more business, more tourists, more industry, more oil and gas exploration, more coal mines. We need more cars and more money, bigger houses and more of them, more reservoirs and more power boats skimming across them. More of us should learn to water ski, jet ski, wind surf. In the winter we need more snowmobilers. We need more highways and the ones we have need to be wider. We should tear down the old buildings in town and build new ones and more of them. They should be made of steel.

I'm not sure any of us really believes this litany of "more." We see how much we destroy in order to get more. We know what we're doing to the air and water, to the plants and animals, to the soil.

Some of us have wished to learn how to live with less. I am one of these. But sometimes I work so hard at doing with less that I make of the concept of less just another more. I become so pleased with my righteousness about doing and using less that I become insufferable.

Often I leave home to earn more money which I bring back in order to pay for what I call the necessities of life. I am already so rich it is criminal. I am this rich with an income that is below the United States government's officially designated poverty level. But don't be confused by government statistics; I repeat that I am rich beyond possibility and belief.

In fact I am ashamed of my great wealth. I am able to sit writing these words, idly speculating about the economy, while not far from me people suffer from lack. They can't pay their heating bill. They don't have safe drinking water. Their house is insufficient to their needs or they have no house. They are hungry and their empty bellies protrude. I mention only the most ordinary of absences.

In the United States we eat and eat and it isn't enough. But it is not our bodies that are dissatisfied. It is our minds. We wander glassy-eyed amongst the aisles of products for sale.

"May I help you?" the clerk asks.

"This is not exactly what I'm looking for. Could you tell me please what it is I should buy to make me feel whole?"

The clerk can only turn and walk away. This kind of counseling is not in the job description.

I wonder at those whose incomes are so much higher than mine. At first I say, incredulously, "What could you be doing with all that money?" Then I look at myself and see that every time I earn a little more money I learn quickly and painlessly how to spend it.

My economy is related to my place. It's possible to live on less in Buffalo, Wyoming, than almost anywhere in the United States. Basic expenses are low and the "amenities" on which people elsewhere spend money are largely absent— in Buffalo there is no concert hall, no theater, no nightclub, no mall. Eating out is generally limited to franchise fast-food restaurants. People walk for pleasure. An evening out is dinner with friends. These are inexpensive pastimes.

Still, I manage to need money and slowly come to realize that were I to learn to live completely without money, then I would begin to know both what an economy is and what it means to be of a place.

A neighboring rancher was tearing down his house in order to replace it with a modern mobile home. He found it not worth the effort to maintain the old place with its decrepit plumbing—copper pipes with lead-based solder— and its wiring that is a constant fire hazard.

I understand why he might be inclined to give up on the old place. Our house, which was built in 1887, is a continual source of do-it-yourself projects. Last night I turned on the water to take a bath and when I turned the tap back off, the water kept running. I turned off the water supply to the house and took the bathtub spigots apart. Inside I found that the washers were disintegrating. The rubber was pitted and frayed and thin. The screw designed to hold the washer in place had dissolved due to the minerals in the water. The next morning when the hardware store opened, I bicycled downtown and found the parts I needed to make my repairs. They cost twenty-four cents. The repair job took several hours.

One day I would like to have the strength to not repair those spigots, to turn off the water and leave it off. Our bathroom could revert to being the pantry that it was when the house was built over a hundred years ago. I would have to build an outhouse inside city limits. I'm sure this is a violation of both zoning ordinances and the building code.

When my neighbor bought a factory-made mobile home, he offered me first salvage rights to his old house. I thought to bring home the windows and build a two-story greenhouse inside of which I would grow all the food we needed no matter how short the frost-free season, no matter how long and deep the snows.

At home, I stacked the windows up in the center of the yard and sat down to rest for a minute. I found myself staring through the many layers of glass as if I were on one side of a wall looking out at the world. As the sun crossed the sky, I moved to follow the shade and found myself on the other side of the glass. Again, I was inside a wall looking out. It was disheartening to think that, one side or the other, I was so distant from the world outside.

There are a million kinds of slavery. It's hard to know how we can do anything which in these times doesn't become a part of our own enslavement. We seem to be slaves to our ideas themselves. It doesn't matter what the ideas are.

Finally, I got up from my chair and, rather than walking again to the other side of the glass, simply opened the windows. I opened all of them so that the light and the air passed unimpeded from one side of the yard to the other. But why did I bring all those windows home in the first place? And why don't I now simply haul them all off to the dump?

If I were really prepared to live with this earth instead of just on it, I'd not only dump those windows, I'd also tear down the house and haul it off, too. Better yet, I'd give the house away and move into the sheepwagon. But what of Margo and Caitlin? A sheepwagon's a small home for three. Still, they might like it, too, and I daresay the new residents would feel well disposed toward us and allow us to come inside on those days when the sheepwagon seemed cramped and small.

Sometimes I talk to people and they pay me for that. I have been a copy editor and proofreader. I have even acted as a judge deciding the worth of other people's writing. That's an ironic twist. Like many writers, I have found myself entering my writing in competitions—for publication, for money, for the right to be read in order to pass on to a more elite circle of competition. In such competition my work has often been found wanting.

The irony in this is not that I, who have been judged unworthy, have simultaneously been asked to judge other writers' work. The irony is that I have been willing to judge other people's art in order to earn money while I deny the susceptibility of art to the kinds of objective standards that prevail in other sorts of work—changing the oil in a car, say, or framing a house, or repairing a windmill.

But one has to make a living. This is, after all, an economy. The best is to make the least living possible. How can we find the lower limit of our need? A man in Japan ate nothing but spirulina for ten years and he was reported to be "the picture of health." Spirulina is an algal pond scum. It's a deep green color. It can be dried and ground into a powder with which one can make cakes. It can be stirred into water and swallowed as a drink.

I have heard of other people who have lived to be healthy old souls eating nothing but earthworms, or iron-rich dirt. Some yogis are said to live on air alone.

These are extreme examples which will not serve most of us. But they point up how much it is possible to dispense with.

But how could we dispense with our diet? Our diet is not a result of our needs; it is a result of our economy. Throughout Wyoming one finds roadside signs reading, "This is Cow Country. Eat More Beef!" Most of us try hard to do our duty.

We don't need the money; we need the work. In 1988 I worked in Jalapa, Nicaragua, building a children's park and playground. For this work I received no wage at all. I lived with a family who, before I began my job, had never met me. They took me in as a stranger and made me one of their own. They fed me the same food they ate—black beans, a little dry cheese which was daily crumbled into the beans, and a thick atole drink made from ground corn. But I received no money. In fact, like a good rancher, I had paid money to gain this work. I had saved money here in the United States to buy a plane ticket to Nicaragua and to help support the international program which had organized our project.

If we were to pay for all the work we did, perhaps then we would do only useful work, or work that mattered to us, work which we could love. When I have loved my work, I have, if only slightly, grown into that love. I have become a little particle of love. That would be a workable economy. And such an economy could go on for centuries without destroying the planet.

In order to build the park for the children of Jalapa, we had to prepare the ground. Some years before, Lion's Club International had purchased one block in the center of the town. They had then paid local workers to pour a cement circle in the center of the block. The cement looked like a fountain but there was no water. Rising from the center of this waterless fountain was a blue and gold Lions International sign, and radiating out from the sign on all four sides were cement sidewalks.

My first job was to remove the sidewalks. With a pick and a sledgehammer I broke the cement into pieces. Then with a six-foot pry bar I eased the cement up out of the earth and lifted it into a small wooden wheelbarrow. The wheelbarrow had a steel wheel which made a loud scraping sound as it turned.

At first I simply attacked the cement, bashing at it with the sledge and pick. I was thinking only of breaking the sidewalk into manageable pieces. After a time I began to think it would be better if I tried to break the cement into large pieces—as large as I could manage to handle. This would mean less effort breaking cement plus there might be some use for the larger complete pieces. Maybe we could use them as paving stones somewhere else.

So I began to hunt for the places where there was already a crack in the sidewalk, or where the original workers had placed a seam in the cement. I struggled to break the sidewalk into regular rectangles and squares. The perfect piece was a square about three feet by three feet. Each complete piece was a triumph. I stacked the cement squares neatly along the edge of the park block.

On the second day as I was working with the pick to extend a crack the direction I wanted it to go, one of the other American workers approached me.

"Hey, listen, there's a huge crowd of old women here all shouting at me at once, waving their arms and grabbing my hand but I don't know what they're saying. Can you come translate?"

"Yeah, sure."

The women were clustered around the stack of cement squares, earnestly discussing the former sidewalk. They asked if they could each have a piece of cement. I had wondered what we would do with this cement and told them that, of course, they could each have a piece if they liked.

I was about to go back to breaking up the remaining sidewalk when I thought to ask them if there was anything else. Though the women were not frail, they were mostly small, older women. How could they move these heavy pieces of cement?

"Well, yes," they told me, "you could carry these back to our houses for us."

"Fine." I still had no idea what they planned to do with the cement.

I lifted one end of the first slab, lay it against the edge of the ancient wheelbarrow then shoved it up and in. It fell with a bang. Without saying anything, the woman who had selected this piece took off at a brisk walk. I followed her down several streets then onto a dirt path and across the creek. It was hard going with the weight. When we reached her house, I passed through a plastic curtain hanging in the doorway and across the bare living room into the courtyard. There were the usual chickens, a pig, an old man cleaning and sorting coffee beans.

"He is blind." the woman told me. "He does all the sorting by feel, then lays the beans out on burlap sacks to dry here in the sun. It is not work that really needs to be done but he does it."

We said "good day," which in Jalapa is to say "To God," and I stepped around the man.

"Here," the woman told me.

I unloaded the slab and set it up on the ground next to a water spigot that came off the roof.

"Can you set it up on a slight incline, please?"

Ahh, I finally began to understand. This was a first-class laundry stone.

For much of that day I walked all over Jalapa hauling laundry stones to house after house. Some were placed on the ground, some on tables at waist height, some on rocks piled up to lift the stone so that one could easily scrub clothes while standing on one's knees.

The next day I continued breaking up the sidewalk, the crowd of women gathered around me, vying for each piece as it was lifted from the ground. If I broke a piece out with a long jagged side, or broke a piece out that was too small, or cracked an otherwise good square, the women became silent. They turned away and looked out into the center of the street as if President Bush himself was leading a parade of U.S. officials who had arrived to commend the Nicaraguan people for their heroic effort in overthrowing the Somoza dictatorship and beginning the long hard struggle to build a new country. President Bush threw flowers to the women and candies to the children. For the men he had a firm hand-shake and comradely smile. You could hear the leaves on the trees rustle in the respectful silence.

Some poor woman whose social position was low or who was simply not very aggressive would end up with the bad piece of cement. When I broke out the next good piece, the racket would start up—negotiations, mild threats, jokes about husbands, who has plenty and who needs more until finally it would be settled and I would load the slab onto the wheelbarrow and start off again through the streets.

I once saw a picture of a communal washhouse and laundry in a village in northern Italy. The scrubbing stones were marble—pure beautiful marble. In Jalapa, Nicaragua, these stones are cement—pure beautiful cement.

When our foreign crew finished building the park in Jalapa, we went to the mayor to tell him that we planned to leave our tools behind. We could easily get more in the States and tools were scarce here.

I thought of the local man who had volunteered to help with the park. When he finished his regular work in the afternoon, he would come to work several more hours with us. He brought his own hammer. The handle of the hammer was a piece of steel tubing. It was bent slightly about halfway up its length. There was no shaping for the hand, no padding where it would be held. It was unbalanced and hard to use. The sweat on your hand made the steel slippery. There was no way to stop blisters from forming.

"Listen," we told the mayor, "there are four hand saws, six hammers, ten tape measures, a box of assorted screw-drivers and chisels, three four-foot levels, and one Skilsaw."

"This is a lovely tool," the mayor said, touching the

Skilsaw with the back of his hand. He seemed to have forgotten that in order to use the Skilsaw we had been forced to run an extension cord from the Army post to the park. We had hammered together rough planks to make a wooden tunnel across the road and run the cord through this tunnel to protect it from horses' hooves, tractor tires and the occasional Land Rover or flatbed truck that came through town.

"Yes, a beautiful power tool."

We suggested that we could have an auction in the square. The tools would remain in Jalapa and all money earned from their sale could go into future improvement projects.

The mayor said he would like to talk with other town officials and residents. "Could you come back tomorrow?"

"Of course."

On the following day, the mayor told us that people had felt an auction would be unfair—only those with money would end up with the tools.

"We could give them away."

"No, that too would be unfair as there aren't enough tools for everyone. And who is to get the power saw?"

Who is to get the power? we thought.

"How about a lottery?"

"Chance is as unfair as anything else. We have decided that the tools will be given to all of the people. They will be kept in the town office. Anyone who needs a tool may come and check one out then return it when his work is finished."

It has been said that economics is the dismal science. My guess is that economists themselves have so defined their studies. In many eastern traditions we are initiated into the way of the warrior. It does not matter if we are learning archery, aikido, the gesture of the crane standing on one leg, or calligraphy. There is something of the warrior in our learning—resoluteness, steadfastness, courage, will.

Long ago in a warring period in Japan, a warlord general rampaged through an entire prefecture. The rebel army destroyed livestock and fields, burned down barns and houses, raped women, kidnapped children, butchered men. Thousands of people fled in terror to nearby towns and cities. These too were attacked and razed.

Finally, the warlord's army attacked a Zen monastery. Having sent the monks away to safety, the master remained inside the monastery in his study, awaiting the attackers. They slashed their way through the gardens and walls. They knocked over statues and portals. They cut open bags of rice and poured them out onto the ground. They burned sacred texts and smashed cooking utensils.

At last the warlord general crashed through the door of the master's rooms. The sound of splintering wood echoed through the empty monastery. The general stood scowling in front of the master. He waved his sword in front of the master's face. The master could feel the slight breeze from the sword's passage.

The master bowed.

"Eehhh!" the general scowled again. "What is the matter with you, fool? Do you not realize you stand before a man who can run you through without blinking an eye?"

And the master said, "And you, sir, do you not realize you stand before a man who can be run through without blinking an eye?"

I don't know if the warlord killed the master or not.

When we pray, we are not praying to the Lord but for the Lord. We pray both that the Lord might exist and that the

Lord might be kept safe from harm.

If you think of economics, you must think of prayer. Economics can be more than the science of sorrow, the art of anxiety. Economics can be our gift to the world, the way we keep energy and emotion in motion. The Jalapa tool lending library is real economics. As soon as I have saved enough money, I am going to buy myself another job and so keep the economy healthy.

Why is it that economists begin their work by discussing the problem of scarcity? I heard one economist say that scarcity is the sole subject of economics. Where there is no scarcity, there is no economics.

If an isolated farming community is unable to raise enough food to feed its members and if there are no wild animals to be killed for food, there is scarcity.

In our society, food is being stockpiled while some go hungry. Millions of gallons of milk have been poured into trenches and buried while babies cry for milk. Farmers are paid not to plant their fields in order to keep commodity prices at what is considered an acceptably high level. This is not scarcity.

Our society produces a surplus of almost all of our basic needs. It also produces a surplus of what are called luxury items, things we like to have but can easily do without. All this surplus and yet we have scarcity. These two things exist together only because we have boundaries.

The free marketplace guarantees these boundaries which are constructed and repaired with money. Using money as the means of moving goods from one person to another means that people can exchange their products and remain unconnected to one another. The exchange leaves no emotional attachments.

In our society, the merchant is free to sell when and where he will, the market moves mostly for profit and the dominant myth is not "giving is getting" but the "survival of the fittest." In such a society wealth stops moving. It gathers in great mounds surrounded by high fences. It becomes property and as such it guarantees the strange possibility of simultaneously increasing wealth and increasing scarcity.

All from boundaries. Not boundaries such as those that separate Mexico from the United States, or the United States from Canada, though these are related to the problem. The most telling boundary, though, is the boundary between self and other. If wealth is piled up in great glowing mounds while fewer and fewer people can enjoy the mounds then that is not wealth. That is theft. When wealth is stolen it must be hidden. And so, more scarcity.

This is the economic model that the colonial states imposed on their colonies. Now as the situation in both the ex-colonized and colonizing countries grows ever more tempestuous, the model is coming home to its original designers. During the decade of the Eighties, an increasingly smaller proportion of the population of the United States gathered to itself an ever larger proportion of the total material wealth of the nation.

Here is the economics I learned from my father forty years ago—the rich get richer and the poor get poorer. Nothing I have seen in my life refutes my father's belief. Only our responses to this fact separate my father and me. My father spent his life struggling to gain material wealth. I am struggling to grow ever poorer in the belief that if I can grow poor enough I will be the wealthiest man in my neighborhood.

My quest is metaphysical and by pursuing it I do not belittle the attempt people make to escape real poverty.

Once a year a group of optometrists from Iowa travels to Michoacán, Mexico to provide free eye examinations to people who have no money to pay for medical services. The optometrists bring with them discarded eyeglasses. Other glasses are mailed directly to Michoacán. In the city of Morelia a warehouse holds thousands of pairs of glasses.

For one week each winter the optometrists work ten, twelve, fourteen hours a day examining the eyes of people who cannot afford to pay to see a doctor. After each examination a prescription is written and the patient takes this prescription to the warehouse where another group of optometrists attempts to match the prescription with a pair of the discarded glasses.

The examination is free; the glasses are free. The people are poor. For many of them, the glasses transform their lives. They are grateful. They hug the doctors, the translators, the Mexican nursing students. They remind us all that God will bless and remember us, that they will remember us. There are small children and babies, young mothers, teenagers dressed in Metallica jackets, old men and women.

Because of these free eyeglasses, the economy moves.

Still, just anything won't do. Sometimes a person comes back with a complaint. A young man wearing a black leather jacket and high-top black leather boots with chains looped around the boots comes back wondering if there might be any other pair of glasses in his prescription besides these with the rhinestone diamonds around the black cat-eye frames. A woman who is eight months pregnant asks if she could have something besides these trifocals with lenses that are three inches square. She only needs a single corrective lens and the oversized frames remind her of her stomach. Thinking about this gives her a backache while looking through the glasses gives her a headache.

One of the doctors wished to remain outside this economy. Though he had been involved in the program for years, he had never learned Spanish, saying that he preferred not to be able to speak with his patients. "If they think they can talk to me, they'll just ask for things." the doctor explained. "This way, I do what I can and shrug."

I've heard it said that early hunter-gatherer societies were among the most affluent cultures the world has produced. They were affluent while living in what we today would call absolute poverty. No one can be poverty-stricken when everyone has enough.

There is a game the Inuit people of the North play in which a small piece of bone is suspended from a string. This bone has been drilled so that there is a small hole in its center. The players of the game each hold a long narrow stick sharpened to a point at one end. Each player attempts to push the pointed end of the stick through the hole in the bone. Several players try to do this at once. The bone is bobbing and spinning in the air. The sticks are clacking and crashing against one another. The players are smiling and laughing. There is betting on all sides. Outside it is dark and cold. Inside it is warm and they are playing games.

These are grown people. Why aren't they out looking for jobs? The truth is, now they are. The picture I've drawn is largely of the past, when there were no jobs. There was only work and play, and so, whatever their deprivation, the Inuit people had enough. Now many of these people live in towns with oil heat, snowmobiles, satellite antenna TV. They're poor and looking for jobs.

I can imagine some of you saying to me, "OK, Mr. Smarty-Pants, you know so much, what do you suggest we in Wyoming do to earn a living?"

Thoreau tells us that "for many years I was self-appointed inspector of snow-storms and rain-storms, and did my duty faithfully."

There is much more Thoreau did and most of it had little more relation to what passes as useful than inspecting snow- and rain-storms. I'm trying to rethink the meaning of the word useful. I once spent a day lying alone in an open meadow high up in the Bighorn Mountains watching the clouds drift across the sky above my face. I can't honestly say that I was inspector of passing clouds. I was less active than Thoreau. But I remember clearly those clouds and if called to testify in court I could make a positive identification of the water vapor I saw on that long-ago day.

My brief discussion of the economy is in the form of A Field Guide to Western Clouds.

Forty years ago on Four Mile, my wife's family's ranch, there was a long low draw between two ridges. There are innumerable draws on the ranch but most are rutted and steep, barely wider than a couple of horses and riders traveling abreast. This one draw was wide and flat. Water ran down from the ridges and the wide draw became a narrow meadow. The grass grew deep and tall. Simon and his brother John put up tons of hay. Deciding to help the already productive land along, the brothers built a series of low dams—maybe dikes is a better word—across the draw every few hundred yards. They reasoned that the dikes would slow the water as it flowed down the draw. More water would settle into the earth and percolate through it underground. The grass would grow faster and taller. They would be able to cut more tons of hay. They would have a series of great green meadows in the midst of dryland. Up above a nearby windmill, they built a fence around a large open area. They would store their hay there.

"And damned if the minute we built those dikes the rain quit." Simon tells me.

"The rain quit?"

"That's right. We haven't had enough rain to cut hay here since we built the dikes. Everything just dried up."

"What'd you do?"

"We didn't make hay."

There's still grass in what has since been called the Hay Draw. There are still wildflowers, lizards, mice and birds. The clouds still float overhead.

We just don't make hay.

Death and Social Justice

♦

I f you work even a little on a ranch, you run up against a
lot of death. At shearing time last year, one of the dogs got
overly excited. The dog's job was to move a group of sheep
slowly through a holding pen toward a funnel which would
force them into single file and into the shearing shed. The
dog was working the sheep too fast. Soon both dog and sheep
were hysterical. The dog picked out one recalcitrant ram and
began working it alone. The ram, running full speed across
the pen, reached the fence and couldn't turn. He slammed
into the fence, snapped his neck, and fell in a quivering heap.
It took him a long time to die. As he did, the shearing went
on. At the end of the day, the dead ram was sheared, too. It's
much harder to shear a dead sheep than a live one.

Once, I helped Simon kill a raccoon. "Why not trap it
and haul it away?"

"It'll just come back." Simon said. We shot it, then put it
in the burn barrel.

Last week I found two raccoons someone had thrown

over the cliffside and into the ranch dump. Some other creature had dragged the two raccoons back up onto level ground and torn the dead animals to pieces. Bits of fur were strewn all around. One raccoon's hind legs had been pulled off and the splintered crushed bones were fifteen feet from their body. The other raccoon's belly had been torn open and the organs pulled out.

One summer day we pulled down the windmill north of the cabin. It hadn't pumped in over ten years and the water in the hole had always been bad. The sheep wouldn't drink it if there was any other water anywhere within reach. We lifted the head off, then lifted the tower itself up in the air, unbolted the legs and laid the tower down on the flatbed trailer.

At lunch there was a violent hailstorm—lightning and thunder crashing all around us. Simon won't work on the mills when there's even a hint of lightning. He's been struck twice before, once lying unconscious for over twelve hours. His body ached for three years after that. When we got the tower down, we decided we'd come back later to do cleanup.

Before leaving, we shoveled a foot of sand out of the stock tank so that we could lift it when we came back. As we were shoveling, Matthew and Caitlin found three lizards. The kids lunged for the little creatures and captured them.

"Those are swifts," I told them.

"I know that," Caitlin said. "Mom kept swifts as pets when she was a kid." Then, both Matthew and Caitlin begged, "Can we keep them?"

I reluctantly said they could have them for a little while to watch and learn about, then added, "You've got to feed them."

The kids whooped and put the three swifts in an empty cardboard cylinder that used to hold windmill leathers. When we got home one of the swifts was dead. The other two wouldn't come out of the box. Later, we had to force them into the aquarium we fixed up with sand and rocks and a little cardboard cave we made for them to hide in. The kids wanted to hold the swifts all the time. I feared that the two still living would die of fear. But they survived.

Two weeks later, when we cleaned up the area around the windmill we'd pulled down, we released the swifts. Back on the earth, they crouched down and sat motionless for several minutes. Finally, they both looked around, then ran like hell.

We smiled then got to work. When we lifted the rusted-out metal stock tank, we saw that there was a colony of mice underneath. They scurried every which way, running for their lives. Simon stomped on them with his heavy boots, crushing the tiny creatures.

In the southern part of our county a rancher has been charged with killing eagles, a protected species. Eagles eat mice. The same rancher has bragged that he never sees an owl that he doesn't shoot it. Owls, too, eat mice. I thought of these things but didn't ask Simon why he was stomping on the mice.

Because Matthew and Caitlin are still young, we make an effort to keep rattlesnakes away from the ranch buildings. On a hot afternoon, we killed a large rattler right near the cabin. We skinned it and Matthew kept the rattle.

Just as we killed the rattler to protect the children, so we used to try to kill our resident mountain lion to protect lambs.

Every once in a while we find a dead cow or sheep. Could be just about any reason for these deaths.

One morning, we saw a golden eagle flapping ponderously away as we approached. Looking back the way the eagle had come, we saw a lamb, mangled and partly eaten. It was unclear whether the eagle had killed the lamb or was simply eating something it had found dead. A group of sheep stood placidly around the dead lamb, paying it no attention. One of those sheep was the lamb's mother.

On April 29, 1984, it started to snow and snowed continuously for five days—wet heavy snow. Cows walked straight over fencelines. Sheep walked up draws until they could walk no farther. They stood until the snow was so heavy in their fleeces that they couldn't stand. Their legs buckled under them and they fell like stones into the white snow. Horses looked for cover, but mostly found none.

When the storm ended half the sheep in the county were dead, along with one-third of the cows and one-fifth of the horses.

A neighbor came quietly upon me as I weeded my garden. Unaware of the other's presence, I suddenly heard a voice say, "Out encouraging one life form at the expense of another, eh?"

We like to think we are God's favored ones.

These are a few rambling memories about the death that surrounds us on the ranch. Then there is the question of social justice related to all this death, to how we behave in life, how we face both the death that surrounds us and the death we help to cause.

One morning after the children's story hour I was coming out of the library with my daughter Caitlin. I always feel a little odd after these story hour mornings. I'm usually the only man there. The mothers seem to welcome my presence but also give unspoken indications that they, too, wonder how it is that a man can be at the library at ten in the morning. Don't I have any other work I should be doing?

Outside the library, I stopped to speak with my friend Sally Gordon whose ranch was seven miles east of town on Clear Creek. As Margo and I did, Sally and her husband Mark took turns bringing the kids in for story hour. Sally and I were drawn together by this, by the fact of having daughters the same age and by the pleasures of intense conversation. We saw a lot of one another. At the same time, we were separated by very different political views. We often found ourselves in deep arguments which both Mark and Margo would attempt to bring to an end by changing the terms of the talk.

On this morning, Sally and I got to talking and somehow ended up in a terrible argument which had something to do with social responsibility. I'm no longer sure what we were really arguing about. Sally was angry with me for criticizing our government while at the same time being a parasite of that government. She reminded me that much of my income came from work I did for the State Arts Council and the State Humanities Council, that these were public agencies funded by tax dollars, and that as long as I accepted taxpayers' money I had no right to criticize.

I tried to defend myself. I pointed out my involvement in social causes, my work for peace and environment groups. She told me that my activism was just more criticism.

"Anyway, I don't see you doing anything now. You just sit in your house or out in that old sheepwagon doing nothing."

By doing nothing, she meant writing. And since it was writing that didn't earn much money, she could safely assume it wasn't very good writing.

I was stung but, raised to be a man, I found it hard to defend myself. I could have brought up my strong domestic record. Margo and I share child-rearing, cooking, dishwashing, all the many household chores. But Sally knew all this. And these are, even by women, often dismissed as not being real work.

As Sally went on pointing out my deficiencies, I forgot to even mention my work on the ranch's windmills. I should say that I thought I forgot. I now know I didn't forget at all; I was protecting that work. I didn't want to mention something which had quickly become sacred to me. I didn't want to hear how the windmill work might be dismissed.

We were both shaken by our conversation.

I went home and sat, unable to do anything. I feared that Sally was more than partly correct. Perhaps I, convinced that my government is corrupt, am only corrupted by my acceptance of work through Arts and Humanities agencies which are funded by that government. I wondered what I could do. Who among us is not tainted by association? What, in our lives, remains untouched by the government? And just how separate can we hold ourselves from that government?

I thought too of how small my life seemed—how private and personal. Perhaps this life was no more than selfishness, an attitude of "I'm happy, screw solving the world's problems." As I sat, a flood of related but not very coherent thoughts spun around in my mind.

First I got mad at ranchers—it wasn't reasonable but it followed on Sally's criticism of my parasitism, my acceptance of government largesse. Goddam ranchers, I thought. Ranchers have lived so long on government subsidies—both openly stated and disguised—that they hardly know any longer which of their work is subsidized and which not. There is federal disaster relief. And there are commodity price supports. Wool supports. Federally set grazing fees considerably below what most agree are market values. Bargain leases on Bureau of Land Management and Forest Service lands.

In our part of Wyoming, the surface of the earth is usually owned by the rancher while the subsurface is owned by the federal government. The government leases its subsurface rights to private corporations who extract whatever is currently considered valuable underground. Surface owners, that is, ranchers, have no legal right to stop subsurface activity, nor to stop passage across their privately owned surfaces. Instead, these ranchers receive cash payments for damage done to the surface—roads, pump stations, drilling rigs.

When it's all over and the checks are cashed, the ranchers then say that everything would be fine if the government would just get off their backs.

In pointing out these financial entanglements with government, I do not mean to suggest that ranchers are somehow less worthy as people or less hardworking. People on the land here work very hard indeed. I knew this from my own work on Four Mile. And I knew how hard both Sally and her husband Mark worked on their ranch but my talk with Sally had upset me a great deal.

In the end, I had no idea who was a parasite and who wasn't. I just knew that no matter how hard a family rancher or farmer works, the market is little able or willing to support economies on a family scale.

There's a small story that speaks to this: two generations ago my wife's maternal grandfather Poppie came, at age eight, to Wyoming from Russia. With his parents, he settled along Clear Creek east of Buffalo and there began working in the sugar beet fields. Poppie's family's beets were sold to a mill about thirty-five miles away in Sheridan. Later, when Poppie was an adult, he had his own fields of sugar beets. The sugar beet business never made any of those first Clear Creek farmers rich, but they got by. Then the Sheridan mill was closed and the beets had to be delivered a hundred and seventy-five miles away to Billings, Montana, for processing. The small farmers couldn't afford to transport their crop to Billings and soon there were no sugar beet fields along Clear Creek.

If all farm and ranch subsidies were abolished starting tomorrow, a lot of ranches here would go bankrupt. The buyers would be corporations who were able to use the profits from other endeavors to, over the short term, cover the losses in ranching. When the land was safely in the hands of distant corporate owners, I imagine the government would then institute a new structure of subsidies to support corporate ownership.

Every time you stop in at the Feed Supply or at the Farm and Ranch Co-op or at the Busy Bee Cafe, you'll hear stories of another ranch gone under, another piece of land bought by Texaco or some other large corporation and another rancher now working as a salaried manager for the corporation. Ranchers who can't face managing land that was once their own often end up real estate agents. Dying of regret, they then help move more ranch land into the hands of the corporations or the developers.

The right wing in our country is known for its outspoken support of the nuclear family and family values. The right wing is also known for a nearly hysterical fear of government activity. It might be productive to examine the places where these two positions meet.

It's clear that if the market were allowed to act without regulatory intervention, without subsidies for certain activities, farm and ranch families would largely cease to exist. How will we disentangle ourselves? And who will go first?

Maybe I should have gone learned and started quoting other writers to Sally. In his essay "On the Duty of Civil Disobedience," Thoreau said: "Governments show thus how successfully men can be imposed on, even impose on themselves, for their own advantage." And later, "But a government in which the majority rule in all cases cannot be based on justice, even as far as men understand it."

In speaking about the United States war with Mexico in 1846, Thoreau made another statement which seems relevant to the argument between Sally and me. Thoreau wrote, "There are thousands who are in opinion opposed to slavery and to the war, who yet in effect do nothing to put an end to them."

It puts me back to thinking that, in a funny way, Sally was right about me. I might be opposed to slavery but was I doing anything to bring that institution to an end?

Some time ago, the ranchers in our area formed a Predator Advisory Committee. This could be a committee to advise predators. Or a committee of predators who advise us. Of course, it really means a group of human predators formed to kill non-human predators. Mainly coyotes.

At the August 1975 meeting, the committee learned that its Gillette, Wyoming, members were displeased about the distribution of funds for predator control. These funds were coming partially from state agencies concerned with land management and partially from the private contributions ranchers themselves had made.

Predator control funds were being used to pay professional trappers to capture and kill coyotes, to buy poisons ranchers could use on coyotes, and to help buy an airplane and pay a pilot and gunner who flew regularly over ranch country to locate and shoot coyotes from the air.

Once the ranchers began to talk, it was clear that the displeasure of the Gillette members wasn't about the distribution of funds. Really, it was that a lot of money—much of it ranchers' money—was being spent and there were still coyotes everywhere. In an attempt to show that the the cost per dead coyote was reasonable, the state offered its predator control program outline. The state representative explained that a training program for the newly hired pilot and gunner was scheduled at the fairgrounds and that with the enhanced skills the training would provide, the two men's kill rate would surely increase.

The November report showed that since the committee's summer meeting 214 coyotes had been killed as well as 37 bobcats, 88 foxes and 17 badgers. The number of coyotes killed from the airplane came to 144. State figures showed there were between 6,500 and 7,500 coyotes in Wyoming. A total of 214 dead ones just wasn't enough.

In January of 1976, after the added training, the pilot resigned after air killing only nineteen coyotes in one hundred hours of flying time. In July a new pilot was hired for a salary of $1000 per month. In October it was revealed that the ground trapper in the Bridger-Teton National Forest, a man setting traps and walking, had killed five hundred coyotes. But the Bridger-Teton is on the other side of the state.

Why weren't more animals being killed in the Powder River and Bighorns area? What good was that expensive airplane? The local ranchers were growing increasingly frustrated.

Picture this scene: a coyote is running across broken ground. Above and behind the animal comes a single-engined airplane. The plane is flying slowly, just above the speed at which the engine will stall out. The pilot jockeys in close to the fleeing animal. The second man in the plane—the gunner—leans out the window and fires a rifle. The coyote hops once, twists sideways and stumbles, slamming onto its right shoulder, face into the scrub.

Sitting in my yard after story hour at the public library, I knew that this coyote's death was a question of social justice.

Often when we speak of social justice, we are speaking of relations between human beings. But the word social must now include relations between humans and other animals. This makes the question of predator control problematic.

In 1982, the Predator Advisory Committee members were told by their hired pilot and gunner that the airplane they'd been flying needed work. "The truth is," the pilot told the committee, "that plane is about completely wore out." The committee could buy a new plane, or buy a new engine for the old plane. Before a decision had been made about the plane, one rancher asked the pilot if he would have a look for coyotes east of Powder River. The rancher had been having a lot of trouble in that area and needed some help fast. The pilot went ahead with the wore-out plane. In a week he and his gunner found and killed one older dry bitch, and a yearling male.

These two deaths increased the value of the airplane before repairs, but how could the committee compute the exact fair market value of the two added deaths? Without an exact sense of cost per death, the committee voted to spend the money to have the airplane repaired.

In the late 1980s, the overhauled airplane was following two coyotes up the face of the Bighorns. No one is sure what happened but presumably both the pilot and the gunner were watching the running dogs, not noticing the mountain coming up fast. The little plane slammed into the side of the mountain, killing both men. As far as we know the coyotes made no attempt to compute anything about values and death. And I'd guess they didn't stop to look at the wreckage.

Those two coyotes trotting away made me think about home—the homes we're born to and the ones we build for ourselves. And that, after my argument with Sally, of course put me in mind of the homeless. There are very few homeless people in Buffalo. If such people come here, the local police escort them quickly out of town, dropping the lone travelers at the freeway entrance and politely asking them not to return. The local churches sometimes help homeless people to move along, too. And then there's winter which encourages us all to move indoors or south.

Anyone walking into town comes down the hill and passes my house. Often when I am watering the flowers or mowing the lawn or wondering if I can possibly plant another tree in my already tree-laden yard, a man approaches me.

"Excuse me, sir, but can you tell me where I might pass the night?"

And I am ashamed to say I don't invite the man to pass his night with me in my house.

"I'm just passing through," he says.

I give the man a little money. It's not enough to change either his life or mine, but it makes me feel better and with it the man can buy something. I don't decide what. My city friends chide me for giving money to street people.

"It just perpetuates their poverty," these urban monied friends say. They tell me I should give the money to a social service agency that will provide free meals to the homeless, or temporary shelter. This way I can be assured that the money will be usefully spent.

But I don't want to decide what the homeless person does with the two dollars I give him. Maybe the money goes for a pack of cigarettes or toward a bottle of wine. My "contribution" won't solve the problem. I'm convinced that the problem will only be solved by the bearer of the problem. And it is possible the two dollars will end up being donated to the Catholic Worker Movement to support a house of hospitality for the homeless.

Throughout the summer the men appear. Some, though worn, appear well-scrubbed and tidy. They are clean shaven and their hair is wet-combed into place. Others present bloodshot eyes and unshaven chins. Sometimes, there's a little bit of caked blood at the corners of their mouths. Their knuckles are swollen, noses fractured, shoes cracked, trousers shiny.

You see how I'm rambling. I think this happened because I was so disturbed. I began to think about every difficult and ambiguous point in my life. My aunt, for example.

For years my family has attempted to help my aunt stop being an alcoholic. She has, not entirely of her own volition, entered several residential treatment programs. Once, when she refused to enter such a program, she was politely kidnapped by family members and driven to the institution where she'd take the cure. Then there was the medicine that made her retch violently if she drank. She would vomit until her body was wracked and shaken. At the end, the dry heaves would throw the slight woman to the floor. The pain was intense and her nose, throat and mouth were flooded by a horrible taste. She was on her knees, tears squeezed from her eyes. If she took her medicine, the family would give her money for her mortgage.

Finally it came to controlling her money entirely. Now her house payment and utilities were paid directly without any action on her part. The family set up a prepaid system at the grocery. At the beginning of each month an amount of money sufficient to one person's needs was deposited with the grocer. My aunt could go in and take groceries up to this amount. No money would pass through her hands. And the grocer had been told to refuse her certain items.

All this has led to my aunt quitting drinking several times.

As the homeless men do, my aunt sometimes passes my house. Even when it is midsummer hot, her head is wrapped in a large bandana. She wears sunglasses and a gray-brown London Fog style raincoat. Her legs are bowed and her step slow. She asks me for money for cigarettes.

One summer day a man walked up and down Main Street carrying a hand-lettered sign which read, "Face of the Homeless." The man wore blue sweatpants and running shoes, a rumpled nylon jacket over a flannel shirt and a Cat hat. He sat down on the curb in front of Seney's Drugstore and let his head fall forward onto his chest. Within moments, our two town policemen and a county sheriff's deputy had approached him. The officers spoke to the man, stood around for a few minutes then left. As they walked away, the man with the sign looked up and smiled.

Inside Seney's there's a soda fountain where the locals gather to drink coffee and gossip. I sometimes buy my daughter an ice-cream cone here and she sits up among the old ranchers and retired shopkeepers.

As they walked into Seney's, some of the ranchers nodded at the man with his "Face of the Homeless" sign. It's that familiar curt nod that says only "Hello" and moves along. Neither judgment nor intimacy. Still, it's an important nod, recognizing the other as a member of the clan.

Other people going into Seney's passed the man without speaking, nodding, or even looking at him. For them the man was invisible. He commanded no more respect or attention than a clod of dirt or a dead crow.

In the Bighorn Mountains above our town is a sacred site called the Medicine Wheel. The Medicine Wheel is a series of stones laid out to form a circle inside of which spokes radiate outward. Academics have long speculated about the purpose of the Wheel and Indian people have been struggling for several years to have the site closed to tourists. But because it's in a National Forest, the Medicine Wheel falls under the jurisdiction of the Department of Agriculture which is charged by statute with managing the land for "multiple use."

The Chamber of Commerce of Lovell, Wyoming, has lobbied for development of the Medicine Wheel as a tourist site. One Chamber plan called for a walk-around viewing platform, twelve feet high, ringing the Medicine Wheel, a snack bar and concession stand, and a paved road directly to the Wheel. The parking lot would be slightly down slope from the site in order to preserve the integrity of the Wheel's sacred past.

At the concession stand one might buy a souvenir T-shirt that read, "I visited the Medicine Wheel, a formerly sacred site of the Indian nations."

On the summer solstice this year, I climbed with a small group of people to the Medicine Wheel to spend the night and meet the Ancient Ones. A woman in our group sat up weaving grasses around a large feather. Once finished, she would hang this woven object on the fence that surrounds the Wheel and keeps people away from it. At one point in the night the woman put her weaving down and walked away to pee. While she was gone, I picked up a log to throw on the fire. The weaving was sitting on the log and I inadvertently threw it in with the piece of wood.

When the woman came back, I nervously explained what had happened. The woman shook her head, smiled and said, "Well, the fire wanted it, that's where it was meant to be."

After sitting up all night, two members of the group began to argue as to whether the Ancient Ones had come or not.

"They were here, I saw them," one person said.

"No. No one came and no one is going to come. They're not coming here at all now."

The argument went back and forth until the person who believed the Ancient Ones had not come said, "We are the Ancient Ones."

The rest of us were silent.

The speaker went on, "That may not seem very fair to the other Ancient Ones. But they're dead, and things aren't fair. There's no justice anywhere."

It wasn't an idea I liked much but, walking down off the ridge, I said nothing.

Last night I dreamt that Simon had taken my daughter Caitlin and me to visit Fidel Castro in Cuba. Fidel was a very old man on his death bed, alone in a locked room. To enter the room one had to ring three bells—one for Fidel, the father; one for Fidel, the brother; and the third for Fidel, El Líder de la Revolución. We rang the three bells. Fidel buzzed three times for us to enter.

We nervously walked into the room. Caitlin went to Fidel, looked up at him and climbed into his bed. She snuggled up against his face. His beard was long and disheveled as if no one were caring for him. He wore hospital pyjamas but on his head was his familiar green fatigue hat.

Fidel smiled at Caitlin and asked her if she'd ever seen the volcano on Hawaii.

"I've never been to Hawaii," Caitlin said.

"Oh, then you must go." Fidel told her. "Hawaii is very beautiful and the volcano is an unbelievable sight."

Caitlin nodded seriously at Fidel who nodded back, still smiling. Simon, also smiling, was standing in the corner. I felt very happy. Then we said goodbye to Fidel and left.

When I awoke I wondered why Simon would take us to see Fidel Castro and why he seemed so happy seeing the immediate friendship Fidel and Caitlin showed for one another. Simon is a warm and decent man but he is also a Wyoming rancher—conservative, a lifelong member of the Republican party, a strong believer in the sanctity of the individual. Personal autonomy is the creed of our rural community. The idea of a society geared to collective social planning and action catches in the craw of many people here. But

Simon took us to see Fidel. And then Fidel said we should go to Hawaii to see the volcano. Hawaii seems to me to represent a kind of capitalist playground. And a volcano is an explosion.

I had this dream following the day on which Sally and I had argued. I had spent that day thinking in a haphazard way about social justice, about my own quiescence, about the future of ranching, about the kind of life we lead here in the least populated state in the union, about that man who walked up and down Main Street for two days holding a sign that read, "Face of the Homeless." Above all, I had spent the day thinking about just how much we must kill in order to stay alive.

More Death

♦

In the course of a long life, my wife's maternal grandfather Poppie has spent a great deal of time dying. When he was in his mid-forties, he was diagnosed with stomach cancer and given a few months to live. Now he's approaching ninety. But death is patient and Poppie can't cheat him forever. Poppie's own son died of leukemia while an infant. It was common in those long-ago days for ranchers and farmers to spread DDT powder around their doorways to keep insects out of the house. Poppie and Grandmom have always wondered if DDT was the cause of their three-year-old son's death.

On Clear Creek where Poppie both farmed and ranched, there was a neighboring woman whose son drowned in an irrigation ditch. After her son's death, the mother would go out every night with a lantern looking for the child's body. Local authorities had found the body and lifted it up from the water. But the child's mother only said, "That is not my son." And each night she continued her solitary search, the lantern light shining in the fields along Clear Creek.

Poppie's daughter Dollie, now a woman in her mid-sixties, has been going every day this week to see Poppie in the hospital. Often she goes twice or even three times in the same day. She sits by Poppie's bed and talks with him. Poppie tells stories of his childhood in Russia and of his own father who was, in his modest way, an adventurer.

Poppie's father traveled north to Moscow and then by himself across Siberia. "There were people," Poppie says, "who would take you anywhere no matter how bad the weather was. They got a sleigh ready, piled huge sheepskins over you and off you went—through the middle of a blizzard. Nothing stopped them."

Somehow Poppie and Dollie got to talking about the woman with the lantern. Poppie began to cry, then Dollie. They cried over the death that had happened so many years ago and they cried for the mother with the lantern. Poppie said that she is still walking through the dark fields, searching.

This week my friend Sally Gordon, with whom I'd had a terrible argument about social responsibility, was killed. As Poppie had, Sally and her husband Mark ranch on Clear Creek. Their place is called Merlin Ranch—for the magician. Sally and Mark have two children, aged four and two. They raise cattle and sheep. They have a little side business selling pesticide-free lamb.

Sally was running west toward town on the left side of the road, the side facing the eastbound traffic. Sally's dog Jasper was running with her. Also traveling west was a seventeen-year-old man in a pickup. I cannot say what happened inside the pickup but somehow it and its driver hurtled across both lanes of the road onto the far shoulder where the truck bounced over three poles marking the edge of the right-of-way then struck Sally and Jasper from the back.

Officials say both Sally and the dog were killed instantly. Mercifully so, we say, hoping Sally's life was snuffed out instantly without pain.

But life requires foreknowledge of death. We are driven to examine our lives as we approach death. We need some time for reflection and meditation. We want to wonder aloud at the strangeness of life and death. The idea that one can, in the fullness of life, be instantly struck down is appalling.

I sat in Poppie's hospital room while he slept. His hands and arms quivered at uneven intervals. Every few minutes he would seem to awaken, turn to his side and search about for something. Several times he picked up the nurse call/TV control unit.

"Do you want this?" I asked.

Poppie turned to me with a quizzical look and let the plastic box fall to the bed. Then he was immediately asleep again. Once he sat upright and said, "You'd think they could do something about the damned noise."

The room was quiet. There was little activity in the halls. The only noise was the wheezing of the oxygen machine and the bubbling gasp as Poppie's air was run through a bottle of sterile liquid on its way to his nose.

The doctors tell us that it is this sound of the oxygen being delivered to Poppie that seems to him to be a cacophonous rumbling noise. The sound is magnified in the tubing that runs into Poppie's body. There is no way to give him the oxygen without the noise, we are told.

The noise is driving Poppie crazy. Once, he looked at me and said only, "It's a hell of a thing." Apropos of everything.

When the pickup slammed into Sally's back, was there a moment in which she knew what had happened before the event was complete? Did she remember her entire life? How does a woman who is plowed over in this way say goodbye to her daughters and to her husband? I can picture nothing of Sally's last moments. A slight shudder passes through me.

In the days following Sally's death, the house was filled with people—friends from town, family from around the country. One night Sally's two-year-old, Ann, was unable to stop crying. She wept loudly, with a choking catch. Once she managed to say, "It's not fair." Now, a little later, this girl asks, "Can we visit Mom in Heaven?"

A few days before her death, Sally and her husband and two daughters were traveling home. They were riding in the family's VW van. The girls were seated in the far back of the van. When they got home, Sally went to open the rear hatch door and discovered that it had been unlatched the entire time. If the girls had leaned back, they could have rolled out onto the highway. They would have been killed. Sometimes I think Sally knew death had been cheated that night and would return, and so she made a decision to give herself in place of her girls.

Sally was a pianist, trained in the tradition of Western classical music. She and her mother often performed in Buffalo. Their last performance, given about a month before Sally's death, included works by Johannes Brahms, Aaron Copeland, Darius Milhaud, Robert Schumann, J. S. Bach, and Percy Aldridge Grainger.

In winter Sally would rise very early to feed cows. In the frozen early light she would spread hay and grain pellets for the hungry stock. Afterward, she would go in and play piano as the snow drifted outside. She wrote to a friend how exhilarating this was to her, how absolutely grand life was to include the piano and feeding cows.

Have you lived this kind of life in which two distant things are one? It is so cold in winter. So much comes to a stop as though it has died. Still, we bundle up and go about our little business of life. I have seen Sally's husband Mark standing by a stock tank in winter hacking at the ice with an axe, breaking through the ice so that the cows can get water. As soon as the ice is broken it begins to reform.

The steel stock tanks freeze up fast and hard. Unless a person is there every day, every time the cows need to drink, there will be no water. The water in the stock tanks made from giant coal-truck tires remains open at much lower temperatures than it does in the steel tanks. Sometimes even in the coldest of weather there will be a tiny edge of liquid along the wall of the tire. Maybe it's the insulation capacity of the thick rubber. Maybe it's the rubber's black color soaking up the rays of winter sun and warming the ice along the tire's rim enough to melt a little stream. The cows lean over and lick along that dripping edge. Even given the magical properties of thick black rubber, the tanks eventually freeze solid and then we're all out there with an ax. Of course this abstraction of life and death is not so tangible a contrast as Sally's piano playing and feeding cows.

I think I understand Sally's feeling. I am amazed thinking of my own life which includes writing poems and working on windmills. I have a feeling of expansion and grace knowing my life can include both things. It is as if I have two lives which have mysteriously become one.

Work on a windmill is endlessly the same—the same

sticks and pipes and polished rods, and oil changes and fan blades, bolts, working barrels, leathers, check valves.

Still, the mills seem endlessly complex and different. As the years go by, each windmill is modified by design or necessity. Parts shear off and are fabricated at the ranch or in town. Shafts bend or give way and are replaced by others that are not quite right but will do. Heads are replaced. Brake cables give. A stick is replaced with a chain. The ground erodes around the base of a tower. Footings are dug up and the tower replanted in cement.

Eventually each windmill comes to have a kind of personality and style. Each pulls water out of the ground at a different rate. And the water that comes up is slightly different at each well.

When, finally, we have replaced or repaired everything we can think to replace or repair and the polish rod is connected to the pump rod, and the wind blows, and water comes out of the ground I feel new. My heart flutters in my chest like some giddy songbird. And it seems as if water is coming from the earth for the first time. I drink like a man who has been slowly dying of thirst, and am revived.

Now I see that in telling you about death I end by speaking about what brings me the most happiness, the most life. In these moments I do not think of the sad reality that we are mining fossil water and that ultimately we will end by taking all the water the earth can give and leaving it barren.

Simon tells me again and again about the days when water ran in the creek beds and draws, about the days when the reservoirs were full.

"We brought the sheep here because there would always be enough water for them," he says.

Already we have drained much of the Oglala Aquifer, that incomprehensibly huge field of water that underlies the Great Plains up to the eastern edge of the Rockies—Nebraska, the Dakotas, Wyoming. There is a vast ocean under our high plains and in that ocean the tides beat ceaselessly in and out just as they do in the oceans at the surface of the earth.

As these tides move, they pull water toward them. The water that once was in the creeks and draws of Four Mile is part of an underground confluence struggling to refill the Oglala, migrating down and away into the earth's dark interior. One day, I must believe, the water will return to the surface. We'll see it rushing along under the cottonwood limbs. The Wyoming bright sunlight will tumble down through the leaves dappling the ground below. Even now I can see all this. I stand atop the windmill and see it all. That moment and this are one.

Writing of the countryside around his home in Concord, Massachusetts, Thoreau tells us that in winter, "when the ponds were firmly frozen, they afforded not only new and shorter routes to many points, but new views from their surfaces of the familiar landscape around them. When I crossed Flint's Pond, after it was covered with snow, though I had often paddled about and skated over it, it was so unexpectedly wide and so strange that I could think of nothing but Baffin's Bay."

And my daughter, looking up at the clouds being blown across the sky in the wind, tells me one looks like a bicycle or a mountain or a Barbie doll.

"Are you sure that cloud looks like a Barbie doll?" I ask.

"Yes," she says, "Look."

A few days later Poppie died. At about four in the afternoon, on Tuesday, he pulled the oxygen line out of his nose. He'd not eaten for days, living on a few sips of beer or water alone. His breathing slowed and his eyes grew increasingly distant as if already he were far from us. For a few days he'd been periodically stretching his arms one at a time high above his head, as if reaching for some invisible handhold. About suppertime he quit breathing.

On Monday of that same week my father-in-law's 102-year-old mother had entered the hospital. On Thursday morning, with her four children surrounding her, she called out in Basque, "Come here!" The four children leaned closer and then Amatchi, like Poppie, died.

The list grows heavy. Three Sundays ago a friend, Kathy, with whom I worked for four years, a woman in her late forties, suffered a stroke and died. A slightly older man, Walter, the father of another friend, woke up with a little stomach pain. By that evening he was in a coma and in a week he was dead. In the Wind River Mountains, a third friend, Ken, has been killed in a climbing accident. And finally, in Arizona, our Tohono O'odham musician friend Elliott Johnson, who plays Gu-Achi style fiddle, died this morning.

Elliot's music was both delicate and rough—the rolling high harmonies of the twin fiddles along with the booming bass drum. How much pleasure the music gave! I picture Sally, Walter, Amatchi, Poppie, Kathy and Ken crowding around Elliott. As he begins to play, they dance—the Purple Lilies Polka, Saint Rose of Lima Mazurka, Second Time in San Xavier Two-Step, Ali Oidak Polka, Sonora Church Two Step. The musicians and the dancers could go on all night— the Hohokam Polka, Pinto Beans Two Step, Squash Field

Chote, Memories in Ajo Polka and the Dawn Mazurka.

This year we had our first snow on September thirteenth. The next morning, following the night's hard frost, the cosmos in the garden were curled in on themselves and their leaves were blackened. I went outside and found among the soft spongy vines twelve large cucumbers I'd missed before. They were knobbled and green, almost spiny. When I stepped toward them, I noticed six large acorn squash. Their deep orange flesh, smooth and thick, makes them my favorite of the winter vegetables. Protected by towering lettuce plants that had gone to seed, there was a large stand of basil.

I quickly cut the basil, astounded at my good luck that it was still usable after the freeze. Then I carried all the hidden fruits inside, setting them down on the blue-tile kitchen counter. The room was vibrating with the smell of basil, the odor so rich it made the air shimmer. I washed and chopped the leaves. Some would be dried, some frozen, some ground up right now with garlic, walnuts, olive oil, parsley and Parmesan to make pesto. I sat down and looked at the foods we'd eat in the days to come.

We eat to live; die to be reborn. Life is suffering, but that doesn't mean it's unhappy. A Buddhist sage wrote that if we meet the Buddha on the road, our best bet is to kill him. That was centuries ago and the sage is long since dead. The Buddha himself is begging sweetmeats from passersby. When he is rewarded for his winning ways, he gives the remnant delicacies away to the birds who shit in his eye.

There is a word in Spanish—duende—which I take to mean the attitude of being fully alive while, simultaneously, being fully informed by the presence of death. The windmills and water offer that to me. So do the turning seasons. With each change, I am reminded of what came before, and of what is coming. In this way the dead are brought back to me as I move closer to them.

Flowers and Frogs

♦

I have been having a romance with my wife Margo for years. I thought about that the other day riding back from the South Hay Draw windmill to the cabin. I'd been doing the usual work—oil change, bolts checked, fan blades straightened, sticks repaired or replaced, check valves cleaned, pipes pulled, bleed-back holes unplugged. I was covered with grease. A fan blade had swung in a gust of wind and hit me in the face so that I had an inch-long cut running from the outer lower edge of my right eye down across my cheekbone. The cut was not deep or serious but it hurt as it was full of grease, oil, sweat and dust. My back, too, hurt from being twisted in the usual assortment of odd positions it takes to get to the moving parts of a windmill. My wrists were sore because we'd pulled the mill that day and the pipe joints had been especially tight.

Pulling a mill means that we bring the entire guts of the machine up out of the ground—sticks and pipes. Sticks are usually joined every ten to fifteen feet. Pipes are twenty feet long. The South Hay Draw windmill is three hundred feet deep. That means fifteen lengths of pipe and approximately twenty-five sticks had to be brought up from underground.

Usually when we pull a mill, one person can open the pipe joints by using two 48-inch pipe wrenches. The first wrench is put on the collar of the lower pipe. The second is put on the upper pipe itself a few inches above the collar. You then pull one wrench while holding the other in place, working the two against each other until the pipe joint begins to open. If the joint is tight, you can brace the lower wrench against your thigh and pull the upper wrench with both hands. If that doesn't work, you hold the lower wrench in place while a second person pulls as hard as possible on the upper wrench. Sometimes, though, the joint is too tight for even two people to open. In that case, you dream up some other method.

That's what we did today. We ran a chain from the end of one wrench to a tower leg, then put a four-foot-long length of pipe over the other pipe wrench. When I pulled the makeshift cheater bar, the pipe turned in the hole until the chain grew taut and I was pulling against the tower itself. Nothing moved. Finally, Simon and I were able to open the joint by pulling together on the cheater bar. Two sweating heaving gentlemen.

After the day's work, I was beat. Driving the rig truck very slowly back to the cabin, I saw in front of me on the road a patch of yellow wildflowers. The long bands of late afternoon light made the flowers glow, and I thought of Margo. It's not that my wife is somehow like a flower to me. Nor that she is a gardener. In fact, though she loves the garden, Margo finds that, as a working potter, she has little time

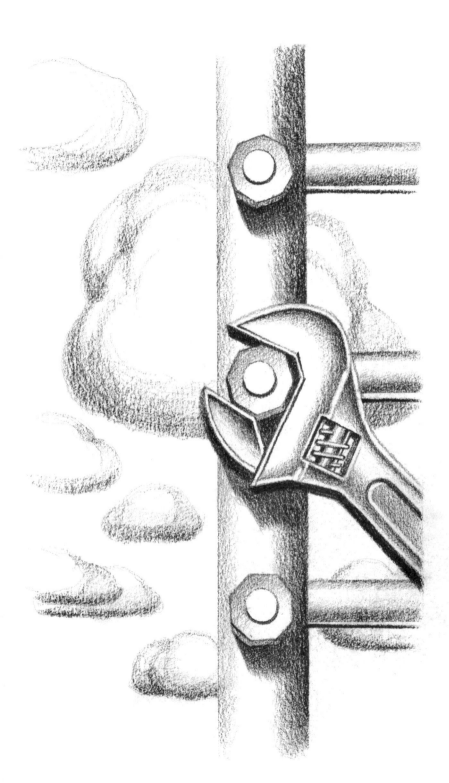

left over for tending flowers. When we began living together, I joked that what I'd committed myself to was ten years of restoration gardening.

The ten years are long up. The garden looks good. Though I know food is what's important in the garden, I find myself less and less interested in vegetables, preferring instead the cultivation of annual flowers. I hack out little spaces in hidden corners of the yard and make new flower beds.

Today there were the wildflowers in the middle of a dusty clay track forty miles from town. I stopped the truck and got out to look closely. I looked up at the sky—the usual spare blue. Even though we've had a wetter than normal spring, it's still dry here. Drier than anywhere I've ever lived. And the ground is either clay or sand. Unmixed.

The flowers were growing directly out of a clay gumbo which, when dry, cracks in a million places and is like cement. When the rain falls, the water can't penetrate the clay surface and pours torrentially toward lower ground. The wet clay is an impassable sludge for a few hours until it dries into crust again.

How do the flowers do it?

They say a picture is worth ten thousand words. Comparing pictures and words is not something that one wants to spend a great deal of time doing. Both are extravagant and wonderful gifts humans can give to one another. As I sit here trying to describe wildflowers at Four Mile, though, I feel a little of why people came up with that old saying. Words don't quite do.

It was a roughly circular patch of yellow blossoms. Maybe four feet in diameter. The plants formed low-lying bushy clusters, approximately one foot high. The flowers were in the bean and pea family with flying standards, wings and keels. There is a great richness in these names of the parts of flowers. Each name conjures up other worlds. There is the standard bearer holding his flag smartly before him. The birds beat their wings in a stiff breeze. The keel balances the hull of the boat and keeps it upright as the breeze strengthens to gale force.

It is as if these flowers are here as a reminder of the long-ago seas of water that covered Wyoming. Through their delicacy and strength, the flowers speak of both mobility and permanence, extravagance and frugality.

Looking at the flowers, I thought, as I have many times over the past ten years, about how the Basques came here and what made them stay. Arid Wyoming is so unlike the Basque Country, that small collection of provinces where for centuries the Basques had taken their living in large part from the sea. Most students of European history are convinced that by the seventh and eighth centuries the Basques had sailed across the Atlantic to what is now Greenland, Newfoundland, New England. They'd done this in boats little larger than a Boston Whaler. They'd lived in the most direct way, facing the harshest conditions the natural world might offer them. They'd come to understand risk and deprivation and maybe they'd come to revel in it, or, if not revel, honor it and wish to test themselves through it.

Wyoming, too, offered a test. It was a land of extremes with winter temperatures dropping to fifty and fifty-five below zero in some parts of the state and summer temperatures rising regularly to over a hundred. The weather could be violent, too—sudden hailstorms that killed any crop a person might plant, overnight spring thaws that sent rivers raging over their banks, summers so dry the prairie seemed to burst into flames which were then carried for miles by the hot wind. Like the sea, the land was vast and empty, moody and unpredictable. In most areas, there wasn't enough rain to grow crops other than hay. The soil was all rock, or all clay, or all sand. This was a place that only gave of itself in the most grudging of manners. The pleasure one took (and takes) in living in such a land must be the pleasure one takes in surmounting the seemingly insurmountable. If you can face the greatest demand put on you, you have succeeded.

Perhaps this is the key to understanding the Basque presence in Wyoming.

I'd meant only to get out of the truck for a moment and go on. But I made the usual mistake of turning off the engine. The motor off, I was flooded by silence and by the noise that is silence—the wind in the grasses, the scuttle of dried leaves across the ground, a few grasshoppers, a piece of wire sawing at a fencepost.

It is this noisy silence that I love about the ranch and its windmills. Sometimes when I stand on the tower of a mill changing the oil in the gearbox, there's nothing to do for a moment. I wait while the dirty oil drains out of the pan and into the bucket I hold. After the pan is empty, I put the drain plug back in and tighten it then wait again as I pour the new oil in. Maybe I have thirty seconds of silence and calm.

The wind riffles my hair and whistles over my ears. I stare off across the Breaks and Powder River toward Dakota and even farther east to Minnesota where the towers of Minneapolis and Saint Paul shimmer. I turn away to the west where the Bighorns rise, directing my view to the sky. I look up, relishing the feeling of slight vertigo, convinced that in this state I could see not only to Minnesota but all the way to God.

I am always shocked and mildly dismayed when Simon and I spend a day working together and Simon pulls the pickup in close to the windmill tower, opens the door and turns on the radio. It has to be turned way up in order to be heard. The little speaker in the door can't take so much volume, though, so there is a roaring that accompanies the music. It's a bit like listening to a radio while a cement truck is operating. We hear a grumbling version of Ian Tyson and Stone Country, Paul Harvey. On Sundays the Basque hour with news and music in Basque and English. Five Gospel Minutes brought to you by the Shining Light Bible and Bookstore.

A few days ago I was walking downtown by the Shining Light. There in the window was an attractive display for General H. Norman Schwarzkopf's book on the 1991 Gulf War—Desert Storm. It's another reason why I'd prefer to keep the radio off. The voice of God will not come across the airwaves in the form of Five Gospel Minutes. And a Christian bookshop is not the place to display books which honor success in war.

Last week, Simon and I replaced the head on the windmill northeast of the cabin in the River Pasture. This well is 231 feet deep and normally brings up plenty of good water. The entire head assembly had been running out of balance and so could not turn fast enough to pull correctly. The new head is not perfect but it runs much more round and true.

In order to put the new head on you have to set it over the mast pipe, a one-piece unit two to three feet long that is attached to the main tower assembly over a part called the stub tower. Once it's securely in place, the mast pipe supports the entire mill assembly—the gears and bearings, the fan and tail, the reservoir and helmet. All this rests atop the windmill tower so that the work of replacing the head is done thirty feet or more above the ground. Worst of all, the mast pipe is not a permanently affixed part of the mill. It has to be held in place as the head is being set down over it.

The head weighs a couple of hundred pounds. We hold it up in the air with a chain hung from the tower of the well-pulling rig. Because the head is much heavier on one side than the other it won't hang vertically. Simon is on the ground running the hydraulics of the rig tower to get the head into the best spot. I'm up on the tower, kind of under around and over the head, holding the mast pipe while shoving at the head assembly as it floats around. There's a lot of jockeying, tugging, pulling and downright suggesting in order to get the head straight enough to fit down onto the mast pipe. A person has to be strong as an ox, small as a squirrel and dexterous as a monkey. Fine, let's say that I'm all of those things. But a person also has to have three hands.

At one point I just about had the head in place when the mast pipe slipped out of my hands and went spinning down through space. It fell into the interior of the tower, but on the way down it hit a tower strut, bounced over the metal and outside heading straight for the pickup. The pipe hit the door just below the wing window. No glass was broken but a healthy dent was put in the driver's side door.

I felt terrible having bashed Simon's pickup. He said, "No problem. Things fall." But he immediately got in the pickup and moved it farther away from the tower. I didn't do this to get the radio turned off.

As Simon backed the pickup away, I looked out into

space and thought a moment about our work of bringing the water that is hidden underground to the surface, the magic of that. When I was a kid, I was taught that water and sky, along with all the natural world, were examples of the works of God. Now it seemed to me this view was wrong, that it made God into nothing more than an advanced child with a very sophisticated set of building blocks. Standing there atop the tower waiting on Simon, I believed that the natural world isn't evidence of God; it is God. I was one step from the view I now hold that God is the mask of God.

Simon walked back to the rig controls and we finally got the head securely on the stub tower.

There are two ponds at this mill. One was about half full of water that had been pulled to the surface before we'd shut the mill down and begun our repairs. The other pond, where no water had come from underground, was also about half filled. It'd been rainy and the weather had been cool. The second pond had been filled only by rainfall and the runoff from rainfall.

The soupy opaque emerald water in the rain-filled pond was bubbling with thousands of fat tadpoles just minutes from being frogs. Each tadpole was about two inches long, its front section and head hideously swollen like a cartoon caricature of the person who is all brain, just a head dragging around its useless body. Or an imprisoned body being dragged around by its useless head.

In his book *The Desert Smells Like Rain*, the naturalist Gary Nabhan describes the reappearance of Spadefoot frogs after the first heavy summer rains in southern Arizona: "The males bellow. They seek out mates, then latch onto them with their special nuptial pads…"

(Those are two words we won't want to forget—nuptial pads. Is that science?)

"...The females spew out egg masses into the hot murky water. For two nights the toad ponds are wild with chanting while the Western Spadefoot's burnt-peanut-like smell looms thick in the air."

I could smell nothing from our Wyoming frogs. But maybe I was already overwhelmed by the smell of the fetid pond itself. The water level seemed to be dropping by the minute. The soon-to-be frogs swam madly to and fro. Sometimes one would rise above the surface of the water then flop back under with a small splash. Often I'd see one of these swimming fanatics crash headlong into a tiny reef of clay mud. A billowing brown cloud would momentarily obscure the green. The tadpole would wallow through the screen, flipping its hind half furiously back and forth.

I stood up and walked to the pond that was filled with underground water. There were no frogs. The water was brown instead of green, rich with a permanent suspension of clay. Around the edge of the pond were the potholes and mounds caused by cattle coming to drink. A variety of spindly water bugs ran over the surface of this pond. But no frogs.

And the cattle couldn't have been drinking at the frog pond as the water wasn't muddied. Were the cows protecting the tadpoles?

The Tohono O'odham people, known formerly as the Papago, believe that rain is more than just water. For thousands of years, the Tohono O'odham have, with little or no irrigation, grown crops in the desert of what is now southwestern Arizona and northwestern Sonora. Like the Basques, the Tohono O'odham's homeland is divided between two countries—Mexico and the United States. When the Tohono O'odham say that rain is more than just water, they mean that water can come to living things in many ways, and each way brings something in addition to moisture alone.

I think about this when I bend to drink from the windmill outlet pipe. Or when I turn on the tap in our house and fill a glass with water. Next to our sink is a white tower-like filter. We run our tap water through this before drinking. Just to be safe, you know. Our town of Buffalo recently sent us a note with our water bill letting us know that random tests had shown significantly higher than acceptable lead levels in town water. We were also told there was no cause for alarm as most towns in the United States had higher than acceptable lead levels in their municipal drinking water supplies.

When I was a child, we drank from the streams in the mountains. Now there is little drinkable water in the mountains above our house. The streams are contaminated by giardia, a protozoan which is present in the fecal matter of both domestic cattle and wildlife.

The Tohono O'odham believe that it is good to plant in January or early February. "That Pap'go wheat," Remedio Cruz told Gary Nabhan, "grows good on just the rainwater from the sky. It would not do good with water from the ground, so that's why we plant it when those soft winter rains come to take care of it."

In his book Nabhan describes an irrigation experiment that was carried out in the Sonoran Desert during the late 1950s. The ecologist Lloyd Tevis used untreated groundwater from a well, sprayed up through a sprinkler, to encourage wildflower germination on an apparently lifeless patch of desert. Using slightly less than two inches of this rain, Tevis noted that one species of wildflower did germinate. Nothing germinated with under an inch of rain. Tevis found that he needed to cause three or four inches of rain to fall before he saw the germination of several species of wildflower.

Nabhan doesn't tell us if Tevis was disheartened by his observations. But we do learn that in January, somewhat less than one inch of rain fell on Tevis's experimental site. The ecologist was then surprised by what he termed "a tremendous emergence of seedlings." Tevis observed that real rain seemed superior to artificial rain in its ability to trigger germination. One wildflower's seedlings were "fifty-six times more numerous after nearly an inch of real rain than they were after the more intense artificial watering."

Nabhan notes in his understated way that "The stimulating power of rain in the desert is simply more than moisture."

At Four Mile Ranch on the northern Wyoming desert, our pond that has been filled with mined groundwater is quiet and still. Ten feet away, the pond that is not quite ours, the one that has been filled with only a few inches of runoff water from rainfall is bursting with tadpoles.

And there are wildflowers everywhere. Bad drainage, clay soil, nearly no rainfall, scouring wind. The land is covered by flowers.

On Sunday my nephew Matthew and my daughter Caitlin spent the day with me at the ranch. We brought a camera on a tripod and we spent the day photographing wildflowers. We could hardly walk without trampling a delicate blossom. Surely there were more flowers than in any previous year. But maybe not. Maybe I had finally noticed flowers that are here every June.

Thoreau tells us that one day he "rambled still farther westward than I habitually dwell." There he supped on wild huckleberries and blueberries. These fruits, he reminds us, "do not yield their true flavor to the purchaser of them, nor to him who raises them for the market." If you want to taste a huckleberry, Thoreau says, you must pick the fruit yourself and eat it then and there. "The ambrosial and essential part of the fruit is lost with the bloom which is rubbed off in the market cart, and they become mere provender."

"Look!" Caitlin called out. There in the middle of our path was a bold waxy blossom—white against the brown earth. Later we saw the first flower's twin plant but the bloom was an intense pink. Later still we saw this flower with two blooms—one white and one pink on the same plant. The flower was the largest we found that day—each bloom about two and a half inches across. The petals opened at the top of a spearlike stalk and formed an eight-pointed star. The leaves were spiny and tough.

Matthew, Caitlin and I spent all of Sunday inspecting the flowers. White, yellow, red, rose, orange, pink, purple, lavender, blue. We photographed each one and, after assuring ourselves that there were numerous nearby examples of the flower we were looking at, we'd pick one representative sample—a blossom and a leaf. We pressed these between two sheets of wax paper and then placed the encased flowers in the pages of a big heavy book I'd brought along.

Only as we worked, did I notice that the book was *After Barbed Wire: Cowboys of Our Time*. It made me feel good to see page after page of cowboy faces covered with flower petals.

The first face I noticed belonged to Dick Shepherd of the

Quien Sabe Ranch in Channing, Texas. Across his nose was a thin stalk and obscuring one eye was a blossom. The blossom was made up of hundreds of tiny bell-shaped white petals. Dick's shirt was white, long-sleeved, cowboy cut. It had pearl snaps, fine stripes on the cloth and a design of tiny flower petals. *Quien Sabe* is Spanish for "Who Knows?"

I've always felt a kind of suppressed rage about the myth of the cowboy. To me, the cowboy is part of an exploited class that has come to wallow in its own exploitation, to romanticize destructive behavior that was historically forced on it by circumstance, nature, and bosses. There are still working cowboys but there are far more adherents to a quasi-philosophy I call "cowboyism." The central values of cowboyism are: a visceral fear and distrust of change; a nostalgic longing for an imagined lost Golden Age; and a belief in the moral superiority of the rugged individual. The most vocal adherents to cowboyism are ex-cowboys, conservative politicians and country western musicians.

The historical cowboy helped steal the land from the Indians, helped drive the buffalo to near-extinction, helped turn much of the interior West into a dust bowl, helped us learn to live as though we had no feelings. And the modern cowboy seems a costumed parody of this past self, a mannequin held together by a silver belt buckle as large as a dinner plate.

A friend once said to me, "If you want to understand yourself, look closely at the things you think you hate. I mean, ask yourself, 'Why does this thing drive me nuts?'"

I was stunned, feeling immediately the truth of this. I'd spent a lot of my life ranting against things that were a central part of me. The cowboy is inside all of us who descend from the European settlers of the West. My hatred of the cowboy image is a kind of self-hatred, a longing to deny what I know about myself.

Matthew, Caitlin and I pressed more flowers into the book. I saw that all those cowboys and I are more like each other than either would want to admit. By day's end, there would be a flower over nearly every face in the book.

Caitlin ran from flower to flower calling out, "Look, look, look!" and pointing at each blossom. Matthew followed her, at first affecting a cool disinterest, a neutral standoffishness about flowers. But soon he too was filled with excitement.

Four Mile Ranch was covered with wildflowers. We lay down amongst them. The stems and leaves, the petals and pollen wrapped themselves around us and hugged us to the earth.

Meanwhile, just over the rise, I could hear the tadpoles in the pond. They were inexplicably turning into frogs.

Culture

◆

One late March day I was fantastically dreaming of the end of winter. I was looking at the Muller windmill catalog and was shocked to see that the catalog listed 164 parts for a windmill. The simple windmill! How could it have so many parts?

I was reading the windmill parts catalog as if it were a sacred text and I was staring at the picture of the fan as if it were a great high-plains mandala. If I'd wanted the combination of spirituality and art, I should have been reading seed catalogs and getting ready to plant as soon as the soil thawed. I could have been flipping through the listings for cabbage or kohlrabi, corn or beans, delphinium or dahlias.

I combined the two catalogs and imagined I might mount hanging baskets around the edge of the windmill platform and grow pansies and marigolds high in the air.

When I put down the Muller catalog I picked up the *Casper Star-Tribune* and turned to the letters to the editor section. The *Star* has the most extensive letters section of any paper I've ever seen. On Sundays the letters section sometimes fills three pages. This is how Wyoming people talk to one another.

I noticed a letter about a bond issue that had been voted down in Natrona County. A special election had been called to vote on funding a performing arts center. The letter writer noted that the people who had proposed the performing arts center had ideas of culture that were fundamentally different from the ideas of the average Wyomingite. That's what the writer said—"average Wyomingite." I've not seen this creature.

The letter writer told me that, "In Wyoming, a country-western or rock and roll concert (depending on one's personal taste) is culture. A night at the opera is not. Rodeos, auctions and gun shows are culture. Ballet is not. Gunsmoke and Star Trek reruns are real entertainment. Modern renditions of Shakespeare are not...The bottom line is, we really have no use for a performing arts center. I think something that would meet with public approval...might be a small natural history museum, or perhaps a zoo."

When I read that letter I thought about my own taste, my sense of culture. I detested the letter writer's view of what constituted culture but his sense of colonial imposition seemed right to me.

When I was a child culture was a word that always began with a capital letter. A big C. Culture was taught to us. Other people, who were both smarter than we were and knew more, defined Culture and then presented it to us. Resistance to this imposition was proof of our ignorance. Outright rejection showed us to be barbarians.

As the writer of the letter said—ballet, opera, the

symphony, Shakespeare.

Another interesting thing was that cultural artifacts were all situated in the past. Culture was archaeological. And the makers of Culture were all dead. We who were alive did not make Culture. A well-educated person recognized what was great art and what was inferior art. A well-educated person was respectful toward the generally accepted icons of European civilization's past. School taught us to distinguish between and keep separate major art and minor art. More important, school taught us to believe these distinctions existed. Major art came from far outside our community. Its existence became another way of telling us we were inferior.

Culture I now know is not about these supposed master-works of art. The masterworks are reflections of historical issues concerning power and dominance.

Here's another way of describing how I was taught about culture: human beings are creatures at home on earth. But culture is located in deepest space, in the heavens which are either immeasurably dark and cold, or immeasurably brilliant and hot. If we are in the vicinity of a burning star, to open our eyes would mean instant blindness. It is a place where meteors come hurtling silently through the vacuum. At any moment we may be struck dead by such a meteor. In order to get to this place we need a spaceship and once there we need a spacesuit in order to step outside. If we were to remove our spacesuits we could not breathe.

And the model of how I now think about culture is this: we are carpenters. After years of building houses for others, we finally come to build our own house. It's not our dream house—carpenters don't earn enough money for that. Plus we can't take too long off from our work of building other people's houses—we have to make a living. But after work and on weekends we are busy hiding nails for ourselves. That house we build, the one that belongs to us, is culture. We come home to it after we have served others.

Indeed, culture includes the masterworks of music and painting and literature from the Western heritage. But culture also includes other music and painting and literature from all over the world, from all kinds of people. And culture includes cooking and games, jokes and riddles, political speeches, diatribes that appear in the letters to the editor section, hunting and fishing, pickups and long highways.

Sometimes in the winter my wife and daughter and I are able to leave home for a holiday. We save our money and go away for a month. Even if we were to go away for two or three months, we could still return home with plenty of winter left to enjoy.

Last winter we lived in Morelia, Michoacán, Mexico for the month of February. Every day we walked together throughout the city. We looked at the houses and shops, the people, the automobiles and buses and bicycles. One of the things I most loved was the way people painted their houses in bright colors—watermelon pink and cantaloupe orange, mint green, lemon yellow. There were so many blues—the blue of a summer sky, or the dark blue leading into a thunderstorm, the gray blue of the sea, the shimmering blue of a swimming pool under an intense sun. There was blood red, peach, bougainvillea, the rare deep green sometimes seen in the human eye. Entire neighborhoods and towns had been painted as a celebration of color. I thought this was beautiful.

At home in Wyoming this intensity of color would be considered by many to be garish and tasteless. We paint our houses in numerous hues of off-white and beige, brick, dust, camel hair, slate. There are some blues and pinks and greens but generally they are so pale as to appear mirages, or harmless imitations of color.

In *The Scarlet Letter* Nathaniel Hawthorne attempted to describe a Puritan holiday. Hawthorne wrote, "Into this festal season of the year—as it already was and continued to be during the greater part of two centuries—the Puritans compressed whatever mirth and public joy they deemed allowable to human infirmity; thereby so far dispelling the customary cloud, that, for the space of a single holiday, they appeared scarcely more grave than most other communities at a period of general affliction."

The point is not that the Puritans seemed unremittingly dour to Hawthorne. Nor that one letter writer in the *Casper Star* believes ballet, opera and Shakespeare are not culture in Wyoming. Nor that I, for example, believe rodeo to be an unredeemable tribute to cruelty and the human exploitation of nature.

When I stand up on the windmill tower and I look out across the ranch toward Powder River, I feel an odd kinship with the angry letter writer. He is so convinced that the separation between "us" and "them" is important and true. What I learn every day is that there are no borders, that the membrane separating me from not-me is thin at most, that the great works of European history share an honorable space with the artifacts of daily life, and that the longer I work on these windmills the happier I am. Then, being happy, it gets harder and harder to be angry, or to remember clearly exactly who the enemy is. I know we have to sort out a lot of problems if we are to have a culture of the American

West—if the West, as a distinct community, is to exist at all.

We need that performing arts center. I think we should all chip in to pay for it, but let's leave out the stage. We'll build a huge hall with hundreds, maybe thousands of seats. All the seats will face in toward the center. The seats will move closer and closer to the center until finally the first row will be nothing more than a circle made by two chairs. The audience members will sit facing one another and those two people seated in the inner circle will touch one another—knee to knee, nose to nose, performing their art.

If the two people are men, one will be dressed in a fine suit and the other will wear greasy coveralls, scarred from a day of work, with no time to wash and change before getting to the performance. If the two people are women, one will be dressed smartly, with no runs in her hose. Her makeup will be tastefully applied with no smearing or blotches. She will carry a slender yet commodious briefcase. The other woman will be wearing a gray dress with a white apron and a nametag above her left breast. Her support shoes will be scuffed along the sides. She will have varicose veins which her dark stockings almost hide. If the two people are a man and a woman, they will be dressed as anxious students on their way to the first day of school.

Part of the performance will include the exchange of clothing. The two people will rise and disrobe. For a moment they will be naked. Then they will be dressed in the clothing of the other. As the two disrobe, a few inspired members of the audience will also take off their clothes. Soon the entire theater will be untying its shoes and unbuttoning its shirts. At some point in all that stripping and exchanging there will come a moment when the culture of the West is born.

Weather

◆

A round here people talk about weather as if it were the major cultural event of the season. The weather is both a personal and a public event, much like a long-awaited concert or a championship football game is in urban places.

The other night I sat down with two friends who were visiting. They were from Wyoming, but four years ago, unable to make a living here, they'd left and moved to Portland, Oregon. There were three other people in our conversation. These three had reversed my two friends' orbit—leaving Portland to move to Wyoming.

All five agreed that though Portland may be a nice city, and the Pacific Northwest a wonderful place, it was unbearably difficult to live there because of the weather. Not exactly the weather, but more the non-weather, the absence of weather. One person in our conversation called it the "absence of any identifiable weather events."

"Out there the sky looks like oatmeal—year round."

Someone else said. "Oatmeal."

"Here's the weather forecast for the Pacific Northwest—
'We can expect highs in the mid fifties with partially cloudy
skies. The chance of rain is about fifty percent. Tonight's
lows will be in the low fifties with highs tomorrow in the
mid-fifties.' "

Everyone laughed. "That's it, alright. And from that
forecast, there's no way to tell what month of the year it is—
could be January, could be July."

A lot of headshaking all around. Then "How you feeling?" someone asks.

"Oh, so-so," comes the response. "Kind of a fifty-fifty
deal. Not so good, not so bad." More laughter.

Weather in Wyoming is the opposite. We ride a roller
coaster bound first for the north pole then for the center of
the sun. One day in January, Margo and I woke up and found
that at 8:00 in the morning, the temperature was 61 degrees
Fahrenheit. Stunned by the unseasonable warmth, we
hopped on our bicycles and took off along the road that follows Clear Creek. The cottonwoods and willow were bare
and skeletal. The warm wind was making the ice melt and
water was pooling in depressions above the creek. The
mounds of dirty snow left by the plow at the road's edge were
melting, too, and rivulets of water ran across the black
asphalt in front of us.

When we were about four miles from town, the temperature began to drop. We were dressed only in windbreakers
and hats. I felt stupid having left my gloves at home. But the
temperature was 61! My hands began to hurt.

"Better turn around," we said to each other.

By the time we got back to the house the temperature

had fallen from that 8:00 A.M. reading of 61 to near-freezing. As the day went on the temperature kept dropping. At midnight it was 36 below zero, a change of 97 degrees in sixteen hours.

This kind of temperature drop is hard on everything but the spirit. Huge cottonwoods sometimes explode, sending branches pinging through the air. Smaller plants darken and collapse in stiff clots. The pressure change lifts small animals off the ground and drops them unconscious. Even machines and stones, those most inert of our companions, suffer. Like the cottonwoods, the rocks sometimes explode. The vinyl seats of our van ruptured, spilling foam into the cold, and the black plastic steering wheel cracked into three pieces.

In Wyoming, we have the climate of both central Arizona and central Alaska. And we have them in any month. It may snow on a June day or be fifty and sunny on a January one. So, like the inhabitants of the Pacific Northwest, though because of the extremes rather than the sameness, we are often unable to tell what month it is by the temperature.

I have ridden horses on days when my boots have frozen to my stirrups. And I've been atop windmills when the heat seemed to draw the moisture straight out of my skin. My face was a porous sieve for the fluids of my body. If I fell, I'm sure I would have lain there in the dust until I looked like nothing so much as the human version of the sloughed-off dessicated skin of a snake.

Then there was the day in August when it rained. Ten minutes after starting, the rain turned to hail then to snow then to sleet.

"May as well go on into the cabin and build a fire,"

Simon said, trying to grumble but happily amazed by it all.

After a decade which included seven of the ten driest years of the twentieth century and one of the ten hottest, last summer was the wettest in forty-five years and the second wettest on record. It was also the second coldest on record.

For the first time in ten years I was unable to grow tomatoes, no matter that they'd been started indoors and were already large plants when they were put out after the last frost. Day after day the transplanted tomatoes stood unmoving out there in the cloudy cool weather. Those Northwestern skies had come to Wyoming—oatmeal.

For the peppers it was worse. A month went by during which all the pepper plants remained the same size. They didn't die. They just didn't grow. It was as if the plants knew somehow that they shouldn't give up, that it wasn't winter, that the light and heat would come. They passed the first half of the summer in hibernation. The corn which often ripens by mid-July produced only small ears which weren't ready to eat until nearly the end of August.

A friend who moved here from Juneau, Alaska, told me he'd gone fishing on the Fourth of July. He drove up the mountain to Meadowlark Lake and put his line in the dark water. It was a cold day and after an hour or so it began to snow. He sat there for an hour longer, his hands growing stiff, a miniature snowbank weighing down the brim of his hat.

"What am I doing here?" he asked himself when his hat brim collapsed and the snow fell to his shoulders. "Twenty-three years in Alaska and I never sat in a snowstorm on the Fourth of July."

After that cold wet summer, we had a bright warm fall with daytime temperatures through October often in the seventies and several times in the eighties. The nights were clear and cool, the perfect weather for producing brilliant color in the leaves of the trees. The aspen and cottonwood glowed yellow and gold. Some of them even went to orange and red. I had never seen their color so intense. The leaves tumbled along the streets and into the pastures. Even the horses seemed to lift their heads toward the warm sky.

Many of us can't bear this loveliness. It's too strange, too out of place. We're convinced that it must mean great tragedy is soon to come.

"Gonna be the hardest winter of the century," I heard someone say down at the Busy Bee Cafe.

"Yeah?"

"Oh, yeah, hardest year ever. Be like the blizzard of '49, or like the spring storm of '84, or god forbid like 1919. That was a winter to remember."

I don't even think the speaker was born in 1919. But he had lived his entire life here and the story he'd heard a thousand times was part of his memory.

The day after this, I'd gone to Four Mile with Simon to work on the windmill just behind the cabin. It was a beautiful day and we took Matthew and Caitlin out of school to come with us. After lunch all four of us walked north of the cabin into the holding pasture to see if the horses were anywhere close. From the holding pasture we went on farther north toward the Bridge Pasture, coming to the top of the hill where we'd removed a windmill tower.

As we stood peering out hoping to see horses, the wind came up. It quickly blew hard and we took cover behind a big tank, twenty-five feet long, that Simon had bought at a scrap sale many years ago. He'd planned to bury the tank and use it as a cistern but we'd never gotten around to the burying and so the tank rested on the hilltop as a landmark and cylindrical playhouse for the kids.

The wind continued to pick up and a dark sky descended from the Bighorns. Soon there was thunder and lightning, then the first big globs of water fell—huge dark splotches on the dusty ground. In a few minutes it was a real thunderstorm with the rain falling so hard and fast that you were immediately drenched.

Matthew and Caitlin screamed happily and ran for the three-foot opening of the tank which was, luckily for us, on the downwind side. They scrambled through the hole and inside. Simon and I followed them and we all huddled there in the only dry spot for miles—the inside of a water tank.

Throughout the American West we find lands of great geographic and climatic diversity. This diversity is reflected in the broad range of human communities in the West. If you want to know our personalities, you should study our weather.

In the West we have often behaved as if every whole was made of at least three halves. Of our place we made a vision of plenty. That vision of plenty has been the blessing and the curse of human habitation in the West. The West seemed to us bigger than anything we'd seen before. Bolder and richer. It gave rise to grandiose dreams of infinite possibility.

Yet the most striking thing about the huge interior West is the scarcity of water. Ours is a land shaped by the relative absence of one of the necessities of life. The plants and animals adapt to this fact. Human beings have sometimes behaved as the animals do and adapted to the climates in which we live. More often, here in Wyoming and in most of the arid interior, we have denied the lack of water.

Other peoples in other arid climates have also tried to deny their lack of water. Throughout the world we find the remnants of great cities fed by vast irrigated farmlands. The irrigators created what has been called hydrological civilization. All such civilizations are gone.

Let's say, then, that water is the guiding rule of our lives and the most important metaphor in our vision of place. Water flows over and around us. It arises mysteriously from the ground and then, equally as mysteriously, disappears back into the ground. We scan the sky waiting for a few drops of water to fall, while the kangaroo rat, living in the hottest and driest of American deserts, somehow attains all the water it needs without drinking.

What we in the interior West share is a commitment to place, a belief in the redeeming power of landscape, and a need to understand how we fit in the web of life. In this way, we are little different from other rural peoples. What distinguishes us is our denial of one of the basic facts of our homeland—the scarcity of water.

It has been said that Westerners are hostages to water. This metaphor related to water is not useful. We're not hostages to water, we're hostages to ourselves and to our ideas. How did we take ourselves hostage and how might we begin to get free?

When the thunderstorm ended, Matthew, Caitlin, Simon and I emerged from the water tank. The ground quickly dried and we once again found ourselves in the middle of an unseasonably warm fall afternoon. We sat outside and let the sun pound our bodies into the ground.

Day of Rest

◆

One July Sunday a few years ago it was hotter than I had ever felt it in Wyoming. There had been no rain for weeks. The sun hung limply in the sky, but for all its limpness, it blazed. The clouds were thin and high. The temperature was over a hundred.

On most Sundays, Simon would be at Mass and I'd be at home. But on this particular Sunday we were out fixing a windmill.

Several mills had quit pumping within days of each other, and the cows were looking for water. Sometime during the following week a neighbor, who leases pasture and water from us, would be bringing more cows to the ranch. As the only source of water, the windmills had to be fixed.

I was high up on the windmill tower making the repairs. Simon was staring up, making sure I was OK, sending tools up to me or retrieving those I dropped. Whenever we needed a new tool, he'd walk back and forth from the pickup which he'd parked twenty or thirty feet away from the tower base.

I'm sure he was thinking of the day when we'd replaced the head on the River Pasture mill northeast of the cabin. That was the time I'd dropped the mast pipe and it had bashed the side of the pickup just an inch below the window. Since then, Simon has been a little more cautious and I've been a little more careful.

For me, growing up in central Arizona, Sunday was both the day of rest and the day of threats. My Catholic father and my Lutheran mother disagreed on the religious upbringing of their children, so instead of attending church they sat silently at home every week, glaring at one another.

Wanting only to escape, I spent most of my Sundays hiding down by the irrigation ditch, climbing the cottonwood trees, wandering up and down the road, and scraping at the dirt in a fallow cotton field. On those Sundays, I received my religious training from nature. Only, as a child, I didn't know this. I remember trying to express my feelings for nature to my fifth-grade teacher, nervously telling her about the sacredness of rocks and dirt. She said this was "the doctrine of Pantheism," speaking in the same dismissive tone she used when telling us about the Greek gods and goddesses—a tone that said these were the beliefs of primitive peoples and children.

I felt alone in my religious feelings. I look back now and think at least one school teacher struck cruelly—by choice or not—at the center of my being. We often speak of the cruelty of Nature or of God but these forces are simply what they are, oblivious to us and our feelings. Only another human being can really be cruel.

Here at Four Mile Ranch, unless we're running machinery, every day is quiet. Sunday is quieter still. It encourages me to listen. The earth seems to revolve more slowly.

At the Gas Plant mill, we found about twenty cows around the empty stock tank. I had to shoo them away before I could work. They were thinking only of water.

A cow drinks around twenty gallons of water a day, but it varies. I'm trying to design a simple experiment that will monitor water intake for each cow through an entire year.

How could this experiment be effected? I could measure how much water comes out of the ground at each well, or how many gallons left the stock tank or the pond. I'd need to measure evaporation and factor that in. I'd need to measure how much water was carried away on cows' feet and bodies, how much was drunk by eagles and ravens, coyotes, deer, horses, pronghorn, mountain lions, raccoons, lizards and frogs. Then there is the rust that begins eating away the metal stock tanks and the water that leaks away. Or the drunken hunters who come in the fall and shoot anything— including stock tanks—claiming later that they were sure they'd seen a deer. Rust or gunshots—either way the water is gone.

I see it would be impossible—I can't even name all of the ways water might disappear besides being drunk by cows.

The only accurate device would be one linked to the cow's swallowing, measuring the amount of water that each cow actually drank. Such a device would have to differentiate water from grass, grass from regurgitated grass, belching and reswallowing from swallowing. This study needs more controls than I can manage.

I'd also like to know exactly how much water we pump each year from the earth. That would be easier to figure out. I'd need only to put a gauge on each windmill's outlet pipe. Then I'd have to make sure the gauges never broke. The important things to know in relation to how much water we pump are: how much water there is in the lakes and rivers under Four Mile; and how fast the underground water is recharged from rain, snow and glacial runoff.

If I knew all of these things, I could finally determine if we are using water or mining water. And if we are mining water, how old is it? Could we be mining fossil water? I already know—can feel it by the look of the land, the growth of the grasses, the ways of the animals—that we're using the water faster than it's recharging.

But my observations don't count. If I measured water draw and recharge with meters and kept accurate records, then what I said about the look of the land would stand up in a court of law, or in a science class.

After climbing the ladder to the platform, I must attach myself to the windmill by hooking the safety harness around my waist with a spring clip. The clip slams shut with the sound of a huge deadbolt being thrown into place. When I adjust a crescent wrench and put it over a bolt, the bang of metal on metal rings out across the landscape. It is as if, because there are so few creatures nearby, each sound must go hunting for ears to fill.

Often the only non-human sound is the wind, but on this hot Sunday there was no wind. Sweat dripped into my eyes and stung them. My hands were blackened with oil and grease, so I tried not to use them to wipe my face. Instead, I swung my head from side to side scattering drops of sweat into the pond below.

My daughter Caitlin had been with Simon and me all day. While I worked on the tower, Caitlin, then just under two years old, tracked lizards and threw handfuls of dust into the air. Now and again she tried to help with the work, but the pipe wrenches used to open the pipe joints were bigger than she was, and she couldn't keep her balance in the slick muck around the well hole. So she sat on the bumper of the pulling rig truck and, with Simon's help, operated one of the hydraulic levers, making a cable go up or down in the rig tower and so lift sticks and pipe out of the casing.

In the afternoon Caitlin grew very tired. She didn't want Simon to help her make a bed for her nap, so I came down from the mill and arranged a spot for her in the shade of the pickup. I laid a canvas tarp on the ground and over the tarp laid a small green and yellow quilt made for me when I was a baby by my Aunt Margie. At one end of the quilt I placed Caitlin's favorite pillow—down-filled and soft, covered by a pale yellow cotton pillowcase, so smooth it almost seemed cool.

With a sigh of relief, Caitlin lay down on the quilt and Simon and I went back to work—he at the rig controls, me up on the tower. But it wasn't long before I heard Caitlin cry out. Then she screamed. I looked down and saw her shaking her head from side to side, wiping her forearm across her face. Both arms were smeared with blood, as were the pillow and quilt. And as she rocked her head, blood flew away from her.

Simon and I both turned toward her. I raced down the tower ladder, trying to imagine what horrible injuries my daughter could have sustained while sleeping in the shade of the pickup on a hot day. I leapt off a rung of the ladder about six feet above the ground and ran to her. Simon was holding her and trying to wipe the blood away with the greasy sleeve of his coveralls. He handed her to me and and I sat down with her on my lap. She had a nosebleed. It was a severe nosebleed but nothing more. I tried to help her calm down though my own heart was beating madly. And I wondered fearfully what I would do if the bleeding didn't stop. At the ranch, we are forty miles from town, and there's nothing between the two but open land.

Caitlin was crying hysterically, and rubbing her forearms across her blood-covered face. I tried to hold her arms and explain to her what was happening, but succeeded only in darkening her hands and arms with grease and adding her blood to my oil soaked coveralls.

Slowly we both calmed down. The bleeding stopped. Simon brought the water jug from the pickup. We poured water onto a rag, wiped the blood from Caitlin's nose and cheeks, from around her mouth, from her arms and legs. There was no way to clean the pillowcase and quilt; the blood had already dried to a flat brick-red. Dust settled and coated everything.

After a time, Caitlin lay back down, Simon went back to the rig controls and I went back up the tower. Every few seconds, though, I looked down, making sure that her nose hadn't begun to bleed again. Simon, too, periodically found some excuse to go over to the pickup and walk by her as she slept. Her hair was matted with sweat; beads of sweat covered her upper lip and nose.

I leaned out from the tower for a moment, letting the safety harness support my weight, letting it alone keep me from falling. Usually this makes me feel completely relaxed but after Caitlin's nosebleed I was preoccupied, distracted. I looked around. The three of us were surrounded by space, not just Wyoming but the universe. For a moment, when Caitlin screamed, all that space was sucked into one point, a tiny place with nothing in it but Caitlin, Simon and me.

Using my anxiety, I had filled the entire universe. Now, leaning out from the tower, held only by the safety harness, I wanted to let the universe fill me.

In 1913, Willa Cather described her response to the prairies of Nebraska when her family moved there from Virginia in 1883: "The roads were mostly faint trails over the bunch grass in those days. The land was open range and there was almost no fencing. As we drove further and further out into the country, I felt a good deal as if we had come to the end of everything—it was a kind of erasure of personality." Cather feared being swallowed by the distances between herself and anything else. To a questioning friend, Cather wrote, "You could not understand. You have not seen those miles of fields...You can't hide under a windmill."

Late in the afternoon, my mother-in-law Dollie came out to the windmill. She'd made supper in town and driven it out to us, knowing we'd be on the mill all day and have no time to cook. I came down from the tower and, while we ate, told Dollie about Caitlin's nosebleed. Dollie then told us about a visit she'd had from a college friend some years back.

After growing up on a farm bordering Clear Creek, Dollie went away to college in Denver. Her college roommate was from New York. The two became good friends, but after college they returned to their Wyoming and New York homes. Though they corresponded, they saw no more of each other until the woman came to visit Dollie here in Wyoming. They hadn't seen each other in twenty-five years.

Dollie brought her friend to Four Mile. The plan was to walk around the ranch then go to the cabin for dinner and to spend the night, returning to Buffalo the next morning. After the walk, Dollie's friend was visibly agitated.

"I could almost see her tremble." Dollie said.

They prepared dinner, opened a bottle of wine, and sat down. It was quiet except for the popping of the wood cookstove across the room. Before dinner was over, Dollie's friend rose from her chair and said, "I have to leave."

"What's the matter?" Dollie asked. "Are you all right?"

"Yes, but I have to go back to town. I can't stand it out here. How can you stand it? We're forty miles from anywhere. What if something happened? There's no phone, no radio, no way to contact anyone. What if I fell and broke my arm or cut myself and began to bleed? I could bleed to death before we got to town. What if there was an intruder?"

"An intruder?" Dollie thought, but seeing the fear in her friend's face, Dollie made no attempt to dissuade her. They packed up the remains of supper and returned to Buffalo.

Whenever I stay the night at the cabin, I try to spend some time on the cabin's small deck that faces east. In the morning, I eat breakfast there and watch the sun rise over the hills. It's a worn deck, quite in keeping with the half-lived-in quality of the cabin itself. The untreated wood has long since been bleached gray by the weather. The boards are checked and warped.

Because the half-wild ranch cats must fend for themselves when we're not there, we leave a large rubber pail filled with dry cat food in a small shed and another large rubber pail filled with water in a doghouse. We've not yet found a way to let the cats get to the food and water while keeping the raccoons out. The raccoons bathe in the drinking water and defecate in the dry food. Whenever we're at the ranch buildings we try to make life a little better for the cats by putting fresh water out on the deck and opening several cans of wet cat food—tuna delight or kidneys and liver. The cats must contend not only with raccoons but with bobcats and coyotes who, as often as they eat the cat food, eat the cats.

Along one side of the deck, we've stacked strips of aluminum siding, torn off the cabin by the wind. Straddling the siding, there's a wooden lounge chair that was built here over thirty years ago. It has no cushions. The formerly red paint is almost completely worn off. There are a few rusted metal folding chairs and some toy trucks my nephew Matthew has left behind.

From the deck, I look down to the corrals and across the expanse of fairly level ground we call the Airstrip Pasture. Beyond the Airstrip Pasture I can see the Swimming Pool windmill. Airstrip and Swimming Pool—they make Four Mile sound like a resort. The Airstrip could as accurately be called Rattlesnake Gardens. Now and again, John Iberlin or one of his boys have landed their small plane at Four Mile on ranch business. And the Swimming Pool windmill is called that only because there are two stock ponds there. Both stay full and I've dreamed of fencing the cows away from one and building a little ramp so that we could swim.

Past the Swimming Pool mill, and on the other side of the cottonwoods along the creek bed, the land rises toward the Breaks, gradually growing rougher, more eroded. At its highest point are the Lizard Rocks covered with orange and brown and gray lichens. Bits of mica lie sparkling in gray powder near sandstone boulders. Past these the land becomes even rougher as it falls toward Powder River seven miles away. These are the true Breaks. I can see much of this from the deck of the cabin and I always stop and look before I step down to go to work.

At night we sometimes stand or lie on the deck and look at the stars. One still night, unable to sleep, I lay out with a kerosene lamp and tried to read a Louis L'Amour novel Simon had left in the cabin. In it was a bookmark on which someone had scrawled these words of Laotzu:

> The way that can be spoken of
> Is not the constant way;
> The name that can be named
> Is not the constant name.

Finding that in a Louis L'Amour novel, I gave up my reading and looked again at the stars.

On the horizon at night are glowing spots that look like huge moons rising nearby, but which are really the lights of surrounding towns. The glow fifty miles to the northeast is Gillette. The one forty miles to the northwest is Buffalo. There's a glow a hundred miles or so to the south that might be Douglas, or Midwest, or maybe Casper.

The light from these towns dissolves upward into the night sky. It's a light that is no more consequential or disruptive than a single match struck in an electrical storm. Yet there's something disconcerting about these distant glows. We are so far from town; still, the towns come to us. Their light reminds us that though we go far away, we are followed.

One summer night when Margo and I were both at the ranch, we stepped down from the deck and began walking toward Powder River. We imagined we might walk all the way to the river, which would have taken several hours. Actually, we stopped about a mile from the cabin at a spot where Four Mile Creek makes a large bend near a stand of cottonwood. Surrounded there by hills and trees, we could see no lights, no towns. If I had been bitten by a rattlesnake, I might have died. If Margo had cut an artery in a leg, she might have bled to death. There would have been no one to find us.

The fears of Dollie's friend from New York are based on real possibilities. The things she worried about could have happened to her. They could happen to any of us out here. It is a small and steady risk we embrace to live this particular life. Something in my present state of safety makes me long for this risk, this possibility that I might go for a walk and never return. If that risk grows too great, I will long for safety.

When I climbed down from the mill for the last time on that day of Caitlin's nosebleed and Dollie's story, I released the fan brake and waited. In a few minutes, water spilled from the pipe. The cows, who had been waiting when we'd arrived in the morning, now returned. Only cows—no bulls approached.

When breeding is finished, bulls must be separated from cows to avoid late pregnancies and then late births.

One day we were on horseback, separating bulls from cows. Two of the bulls took off in opposite directions so Simon and I split up, each following one bull. Simon got around in front of his bull, turned it and had persuaded it to approach the open gate through which the bull was meant to walk. At the gate, though, the bull turned and charged back the way he'd come and into a cottonwood grove. Bulls know a horse and rider are at a disadvantage in the trees. It's hard to move fast—there are overhanging dead limbs waiting to slash a rider's face and arms. There are downed branches waiting to tangle up a horse's feet.

The bull ran behind a tree and stopped there. Simon's horse walked slowly toward the tree from the opposite side. When the horse had just about reached the tree, the bull leapt and, whirling around the tree trunk, charged the horse, ramming him head-on. The bull was dehorned, but even so its charge was terrifying. The horse planted his hind legs and, without going down, took the blow, a jarring thunderous whack, in the lower neck and chest. Then Simon and the horse turned and trotted away.

"When a bull's in that kind of a mood, it's better to just leave him alone for a while with his thoughts," Simon later told me.

As Simon was riding away, I was riding slowly along the fence behind the second bull. He had almost walked through the gate when suddenly he kicked furiously and rose right over the fence, cracking a post in his flight and almost taking it with him. I galloped to the gate and into the second pasture pursuing a cloud of dust. As I approached the bull, he turned and charged, managing to catch my horse in the flank. When the bull jerked his head up, he flipped the horse over. I was caught for a minute under my horse and badly bruised. Had the bull not been dehorned, the horse might have been dead.

That was another day. Today was Sunday, a long hot day in summer. We were working to guarantee water for bulls and cows to drink. For horses and humans, too. For every thirsty creature.

Simon and I were gathering the tools and lowering the tower on the rig truck. Once everything was arranged, we'd head for the cabin and barn where we'd put the machinery away. After that, we planned to go to town for the night.

Dollie had made up a covered plate for Caitlin, set it in the back of the pickup, and packed up the leftovers from the picnic supper. Then she'd driven away, wanting to get to Buffalo before dark.

As I was shoving the safety harness into its spot in the pickup's tool boxes, I heard Caitlin waking up. I pulled off my coveralls and sat down with her.

"How ya feeling, sweetie?" I asked.

"OK."

We joked a little about her nosebleed, then shared an apple and some corn chips. She said she'd eat real supper on the way home in the truck. We decided to stay at the mill long enough to watch the sun settle down over the Bighorns. The clouds made long horizontal bands, orange at first then going to rose. The intense light of the long shadows dulled and it began to grow dark. We got in the truck and drove slowly away.

Strange Communion:
NOTES OF A NON-HUNTER

S ome years ago, on a day near Thanksgiving, an unseasonably warm day that drew me outside on my bicycle, I left the ranch behind, pedaling west toward the Bighorn Mountains. Near the town of Story, I saw my friend Dainis Hazners in a field, carefully stalking birds. Dainis was slogging through underbrush and bits of old snow and ice. Some of the snow had melted and created substantial areas of boggy sodden ground. When Dainis saw me, he waved and called me over. We began to talk about hunting. He told me that it was only through the hunt, only through the deliberate act of killing for food that we understand life on this earth. He said that I could never be a mature human being if I didn't hunt. I was condemned to remain childlike in some important way.

I told Dainis that, though I had been a vegetarian for twenty years, I too had killed animals. There was the great blue heron that had collided feet first with the windshield of a large truck. The bird's legs were crumpled beyond repair and its chest was smashed. There was also the family cat that had been hit by a car and come home trailing its intestines in a long stream behind it.

Dainis frowned at me and said with some vehemence, "That's not it at all. Those are mercy killings. They have nothing to do with what can and must be learned only through hunting."

We talked some more, both about hunting and other things—the weather, friends, a proposed real estate development we both opposed—then Dainis stepped off across the oozing earth. I got back on my bicycle and pedaled away, thinking about his words, "condemned to remain child-like...never be a mature human being." I didn't believe that and I realized that what was missing for me in Dainis's view of hunting was necessity.

After killing a seal, an Inuit hunter took into his mouth a bit of ice. As the ice melted, the hunter placed his mouth over the seal's mouth and let the water trickle from human to seal. On the Northwest coast native fishermen carefully laid out the bones of the first salmon caught so that the fish might continue its journey in the spirit world. In these cases the careful handling of the killing allowed the hunters to feel their oneness with the animal world, with the spirits, and with the continuity of the natural cycles. For these people, hunting, first a necessity for their survival, became a way of praising and finding meaning in killing. That was the order of the events—first the hunt and second the finding of some way to give meaning to the hunt. Early hunting peoples did not seek a spiritual relationship with the world and so go hunting. They did what was necessary. When necessity is deleted from hunting, the hunt becomes sport and, in killing, there can be no sport.

Years later, I mentioned these thoughts to Dainis, emphasizing the idea of necessity. He said, "Yes, I think you're right. I don't feel quite the same way now as I did then about hunting." I wondered if I could face my own life—the irony of being a vegetarian ranch hand—and admit to such change.

One day in autumn, my wife Margo and I were moving cows at Four Mile. We had ridden horseback about eleven miles, finally coming, in late afternoon, south down a long narrow draw into the pasture where we'd leave the cows that night. We rode about fifty feet apart at the end of the long line of animals. We were covered by a film of dust. The sun was beginning to set and its light was intense and rich, giving to everything an incised burnished look.

Margo called to me and when I turned toward her and the setting sun, I saw only the dark silhouette of a horse and rider outlined in gold. I lifted my hand to shade my eyes, and Margo's face came into view. She smiled.

"It's beautiful."

"Yes, it is."

Then she said, "It's too bad it's about killing." And we rode on down the draw.

Earlier that year, Margo and I had gone to visit my Uncle Eric on his ranch in eastern Oregon. During the visit, Eric and I had worked together worming bulls. We had to get the bulls into a small corral then move them down a funnel until they were in a narrow runway leading to a squeeze chute. As each bull moved toward the squeeze chute, we readied ourselves.

It's impossible to tell if a bull approaching the chute will suddenly run, hoping to get through before the steel side gates can be slammed up against his body. Or if the bull will balk. Or if he will try to turn around. Now and again a bull will manage to get himself twisted into a horseshoe shape in the chute, his head and rump facing the same way, his body wedged in so that he cannot move. And once in a great while a bull will throw himself over backwards.

We had just missed two bulls in a row, slamming the sides of the squeeze chute up too late so that the animals were only partly and insecurely held in place. We were thus forced to let them out and move them back into the corral to start over. This is a bad practice, for when a bull learns that it is possible to successfully run the gauntlet, he has a tendency to try harder and to teach other bulls.

My uncle and I were both sweating and sore. He looked at me and said, "It's you vegetarians driving ranchers out of business."

There's plenty of work on a ranch that goes along with worming bulls and maintaining water wells—fencing; gathering, branding and ear-tagging cows; shearing and docking sheep. I like to think I am nurturing, but all of my work means death for domestic animals. I've called my life as a vegetarian ranch hand an irony, but it's more serious than that. I must look clearly at the ways that my life is implicated in others' deaths. I strive to do only as much killing as is necessary; still, I'm killing.

Raising sheep and cattle for slaughter is not hunting, though, and neither is mining fossil water. Most would seek to distinguish between these various kinds of killing. Paul Shepard, in writing the introduction to Jose Ortega y Gasset's *Meditations on Hunting* states that the hunter

understands that the domesticated animal is degenerate and the cornfield is static.

Still, the farmer and rancher have their own view. Of a newcomer who wanted to go duck hunting on his neighbor's land, a Crook County, Wyoming, rancher said, "You spend about as much money for one shotgun shell as you do for one rifle shell. One rifle shell will down an elk and feed you for a year. One duck will feed you for a meal, providing that you can stand the smell."

Whether you raise cows or hunt elk, you kill to put food on the table. That's the rancher's view, and, as a vegetarian, it's mine. It's not Shepard's view. He tells us that the hunt is not primarily an economic venture. Feedlot beef and alfalfa sprouts may feed our bodies but there is something else our soul requires. Anthropological studies, Shepard says, reveal that human "social, intellectual and even ethical traits came into existence in an ecological context, associated with the human animal's niche and, more particularly, his place in Paleolithic food webs." Such human beings are adapted to "the ceremonial hunting of large, dangerous mammals living in herds in open country." Ninety-nine percent of human life has been lived as hunter. We are meant to be hunters. Shepard even states that human hands and legs are designed for the hunt and once we accept that, we will be able to find in our heads the mind that has always been there—the mind of the hunter.

But I don't live in the Paleolithic. And my hands and legs seem as well designed to pull a breech calf as to hunt.

I want to believe that my choices arise from reverence for life but even that old phrase is up for debate. Shepard, too, speaks of reverence for life, saying that "only the hunter confronts this question with full human dignity, beginning with an affirmation of his ecology rather than its denial."

He goes on to say that essential human nature is inseparable from the hunting and killing of animals and from these come the most advanced aspects of human behavior. Through hunting, he concludes, we experience "the Dionysian moment of unity and freedom in ecstasy of intense release unknown to herbivores, based on the recognition of the perpetuation of life at the moment of the kill."

I think what Shepard says is inflated but possible. Though the hunt destroys life, it may also intensify and embody the mystery of life. It may join us physically and spiritually to those we have killed. When we eat the flesh of an animal we have killed, we are granted the opportunity to become that animal. Our bond to all life can be strengthened, clarified and intensified by hunting, by the act of consciously stalking and murdering an animal.

But there are many ways for us to enter fully the mystery of life and death and some of us cannot enter that mystery through the hunt. For some of us the hunt can only be a degradation of both ourselves and our prey.

Four Mile is home not only to domestic stock but to deer, pronghorn, coyotes, rattlesnakes, raccoons, owls, hawks, bobcats, and a resident mountain lion. I know this lion and admire it. Once we might have tried to kill the mountain lion. We no longer consider killing every predator on the ranch the right solution to predation problems. Perhaps one could say we're protecting the web of life. At the same time, our limited protection of some predators translates directly into death for domestic animals. Those half-wild cats around the ranch buildings, for example. Aside from the very quick and the very clever, most of them don't last very long. One could say I shouldn't keep domestic cats at the ranch, but without the cats, the ranch buildings would be overrun with mice.

At Four Mile I regularly see eagles, sometimes several at a time. I once saw six together, both Golden and Bald. There's a spot behind our cabin where the hills rise away to the west. At the top is a mound of shale. Looking farther west, one sees the Bighorn Mountains rising to over thirteen thousand feet. To the north and south the land rolls away in a series of ridges. The eagles often fly there and I have now and again been able to sit for long periods watching their flight. It is not through bringing them out of the sky that I come to understand them.

I like to think I have gone some distance toward entering the mind of the other—of the horses, cows and sheep with whom I work, of the bobcats, mountain lions, coyotes, pronghorn, deer and raccoons I sometimes see around the place. I'm not sure, though. We have barely penetrated the secret places of our own human hearts. It may be that none of us knows the inner lives of even our closest animal companions, much less the more distant wild or "lower" animals—the elk, deer, turkey, spiders, or snakes. We cannot describe thought and feeling in the non-human animal worlds. Not knowing what an animal's experience of its life is, I am reluctant to accept that we may without consequence shorten those lives.

Life wants to live. This want is both structural—built into organisms—and, in humans, psychological. It may be psychological in other living things, too. For now, we only know that there is some drive in all living things to remain alive.

I pass the days and, now and again, I am lucky enough to get a glimmer of the oneness of our lives: one of our horses cut her right hind leg quite badly. Each day this week we have had to irrigate the open wound with an antibiotic wash. This stings and the horse, an untrained two year old, shies from the medicine. She lifts her leg and flops her hoof at the ankle. She skips sideways and if we don't snub her to a post, she tries to run. Yet as I stand speaking to her, I can see the muscles in her neck relax slightly. She allows me to proceed. When we finish irrigating the raw wound, we give her two shots—ten milligrams each—of penicillin. She jerks back when the needle enters her flesh. She eyes me suspiciously and pushes my head with her nose. Still, she comes to us when we return each day.

How can I begin to approach this horse's life? I extrapolate from what I know. How do I think, feel, move in the world? What does it mean to me to be alive? Rachel Carson said that in writing of a prey animal fleeing in fear from a predator, she knew there was no scientific basis for the use of the word fear. She used it though, because the animal behaved in exactly the same way a human would when feeling fear. Saying that the behavior was based on fear was the only way to make it intelligible, to treat the animal with ethical consideration. We know so little about the thoughts and feelings of other creatures; modesty calls upon us not to underestimate their lives. In a letter written near the end of her life, Carson spoke of what she would remember of the Maine Coast. Above all, "the monarchs, that unhurried drift of one small winged form after another, each drawn by some invisible force."

Each of us confronts mortality—our own and that of

others. It does not matter if we are hunters or not. We know that while energy may go on for a very long time indeed, we will not, and neither will our neighbors on this planet. When I eat a carrot, I am as aware of the issues of life and death as I am when I take a bite of elk stew. I must also admit that I feel closer to creatures with central nervous systems, those with whom I seem to have direct communication. Aware that I must kill something, I kill carrots. Even the smallest death reveals the magnitude and seriousness of life. There is no justification for killing those with whom we share life. There is only necessity, and that is not the same as justification.

In *Coming into the Country*, John McPhee wrote about his fear of grizzly bears, and of his uncertainty about how to comport himself when in grizzly country. Many people counseled McPhee never to go into the woods without a high-powered rifle. If he had an encounter with a bear, he was to shoot it. Other people told McPhee that he shouldn't carry a gun. A person who is not skilled in the use of a rifle and who tries to use one in a time of danger and confusion is as likely to shoot himself as he is to shoot his prey. A grizzly who is shot and not killed will become enraged and often maul its assailant even when it originally had not planned to do so. Some people suggested to McPhee that there is a subtle difference in the behavior and attitude of a person who carries a rifle, that grizzlies can sense this difference and that they don't like the spirit of the gun-carrying human. They are more likely to attack the gun carrier than the unarmed person. Perhaps a gun-carrying human smells bad.

Once, after a gunless and anxiety-filled hike through grizzly territory, McPhee arrived safely at the cabin of an acquaintance who then served his weary and relieved guest grizzly steaks for dinner. McPhee ate and wrote of the meal: "The grizzly was tender with youth and from a winter in the den. More flavorful than any wild meat I have eaten, it expanded my life list—muskrat, weasel, deer, moose, musk-ox, Dall sheep, whale, lion, coachwhip, rattlesnake...grizzly. And now a difference overcame me with regard to bears. In strange communion, I had chewed the flag, consumed the symbol of the total wild, and from that meal forward, if a bear should ever wish to reciprocate, it would be only what I deserve."

I sing when I'm in grizzly country. Now I wonder if I'd better learn which songs grizzlies like.

The most beautiful passage I've read on the dilemma of the man who kills to live was written by John Haines in his book *The Stars, the Snow, the Fire*. When he first began to trap for a living on the land around Richardson, Alaska, Haines caught a fox. A bullet hole would spoil the pelt, and so the animal had to be killed in some other way. Experienced trappers had instructed Haines to take a stick and strike the animal a sharp blow on the nose in order to knock it out. With some trepidation he did this, and, just as he had been told, the fox was out cold. All that remained was the killing:

I quickly kneeled down in the snow. I seized the uncon-scious fox by his forelegs and drew him into my lap. Holding him there with one hand, I grasped his muzzle tightly in my other hand and twisted his head as far around as I could, until I felt the neckbone snap, and a sudden gush of blood came from his nostrils. A shudder ran through the slender, furred body, and then it was still.

I released him and got to my feet. I stood there, looking down at the soiled, limp form in the snow, appalled at what I had done. This is what trapping meant when all the romance was removed from it: a matter of deceit and steel set against hunger. But I had overcome my fear, and I felt something had been gained by that.

And something had been lost. This is how it is, not only trapping foxes but raising cows to sell as beef, or sheep as mutton. Or hunting elk for one's own table through the winter. Or pulling up carrots.

One day while working at the ranch, I asked Simon, "When was the last time you went hunting?"

"About six years ago, Stan Borchaski and I went out elk hunting but we hoped we wouldn't see any animals. We planned to spend some time out of doors, walking, taking pictures. Seemed like every step we took we bumped into an elk. 'You see that?' Stan would ask me. 'No, I didn't see anything.' 'Neither did I,' he'd say. We had to keep turning away and walking the other direction to avoid the damn elk."

"And when was the last time you hunted before that?"

"Oh, maybe another five years earlier."

"But you hunted when you were younger?"

"Yes, every year, we'd go out and get a deer or elk for meat through the winter."

"Why'd you quit?"

"Well, first off when we got fences and so didn't have herders at the ranch it got to where that fall time we just couldn't get away. And then I got to where I didn't want to do any more killing. I'd killed everything I wanted to."

When questioned about the morality of killing animals

for food, Buddhists have suggested that such killing is not necessarily immoral. Still, it brings disharmony into the world and as such should be avoided. There is already so much pain in the world; a person should try to do the least harm possible.

But what about John McPhee's grizzly experience? McPhee said that as he was enlarged by eating a grizzly bear, so too would a bear be enlarged by eating him. McPhee ate that grizzly and said that he had entered into "strange communion."

There is a deep relationship between the communion of the hunter and the Holy Communion of the church, some ancient link between Christianity and the hunting peoples who lived and killed for millennia before Christ walked on this earth. I don't know if the eating and drinking of Christ is the reinforcement of the sacred hunt, or if it is meant to replace the hunt, to maintain the power of the hunt while not requiring the actual butchery. Clearly, one kind of food has replaced another. And in the fast before Communion, there is something about not mixing spirit food with material food, about not confusing the two realms.

Perhaps the hunt is a way to have communion with the natural world. Perhaps painting a picture of that world— even a poorly executed, clumsy little painting—is a way to have communion. Perhaps writing a poem, or only sitting.

In late May or early June, I plant my garden. I get up early and go to work. The closest neighbors are asleep and the road is quiet. I crumble the cool, dark, moist earth, making it fine, then I plant the seeds. A few birds quit singing and fly down from the hedge to watch. They are looking for worms, grubs, other insects that might be exposed by my work. But I pretend the birds have come down not to the worms, but to me. I explain what I'm doing. Sometimes the birds cock their heads and listen to the entire talk. Sometimes they fly away while I'm in mid-sentence.

Long ago human beings felt kinship and solidarity with only those other humans closest to them—members of their family, their clan, their village. As time passed, our circles of kinship widened and, though our behavior has often flown in the face of our beliefs, we have seen that our community includes all human beings. Now it is time to widen the community again: dogs, dolphins, mayflies, tarantulas, bears— each must be welcomed and made at home.

Henry David Thoreau was asked to send a particular turtle to zoologists at Harvard. The turtle would be a "specimen." Thoreau dispatched the animal but he didn't feel good about it, saying that however his little specimen might serve science he and his relation to nature would be the worse for what he had done. "I pray," Thoreau wrote, "that I may walk more innocently and serenely through nature. No reasoning whatever reconciles me to this act."

I too have sent my little specimens for one cause or another and so am, like Thoreau, an unreconciled brother to all who have killed. Still, I struggle to do less killing, to treat animals with the tenderness and consideration that has formerly been reserved for our fellow humans. If there is transcendent illumination to be had, it must be gained not from the taking of life but from the offering of it.

Bicycle

♦

ohn Lane was visiting and we decided to spend a day bicycling to Four Mile. Going the back way, it's about fifty-five miles with a slow transition from town to country on Old US 87 and rode south from Buffalo. Nine miles east of town, we turned onto the Trabing Road and rode east past the long defunct Colorado Flats irrigation scheme. This land along Trabing Road is gently rolling. It's the earth's poor imitation of the sea. The grass is low and shimmers in the sun. When the wind blows you can mark the currents in the waving of brown and green.

It looks like it'd be good grazing—no draws for sheep to walk up in a storm and bunch until they die, no steep ravines and holes for cows to fall into. But the soil is thin. Overgrazed even slightly, it blows away like money in a land developer's nightmare.

There are a couple of lines that have been in my head for over a year now—"Tell me it's beautiful where you come from. I want to know it's beautiful."

I don't know where these lines came from nor why they keep spinning around in my thoughts. They feel dreamy, not booklike. It's as though a stranger grabbed me on the street, pulled my face close and whispered such words to me in the fullness of the day.

I'm begging someone to tell me some other place is beautiful, and someone is begging me to say the same thing of this place. This is something about our longing for travel coupled with our longing to stay in the same place.

Right now, riding this bicycle, it's beautiful where I come from.

Kim Fadiman, who has been called Mr. Wizard for grown-ups, and who makes part of his living setting avalanche charges at the Teton Village ski area, used to travel around Wyoming giving a talk on our conception of beauty. He compared the landscape around Jackson—the Tetons, generally held to be beautiful—with the landscape around Gillette—sage grassland, generally held to be not beautiful. In fact, once I heard someone say of Gillette and the surrounding plains—"It's so fucking ugly you want to blow the whole thing up." That's strong language. On the surface, it seems to be an argument in favor of the power of beauty in our lives.

But I'm not sure: Jackson's mountains, Gillette's prairie. We're asked to ponder the question of whether or not there is an inherent beauty only in certain landscapes. We are forced to define beautiful.

Chip Rawlins, who spent several years collecting snow in the Wind River Mountains in order to monitor air pollution levels, has said that he was changed by his work in the Wind Rivers. In his book *Sky's Witness* he wrote that the mountains are "a place that demands to be noticed."

Rawlins felt that he was changed, not because he wanted to be, but because the mountains demanded it. "Notice us!" they shouted, then "Change!"

Later Rawlins said, "I think the same process can take place in unspectacular country, out of a will to know something besides oneself."

But Rawlins seemed to recognize this possibility only after the change. I have had this experience—as though I had to be hit over the head by the "spectacular" before I could see this same "spectacular" in the "unspectacular."

Is it because the mountains are big that they demand to be noticed? Or because they are dangerous? I'm unsure but I think I know how Rawlins felt. The mountains draw me in, too—the high peaks lost in the clouds, the glaciers, the massive moraines left from past glaciers, the streams tumbling wildly down to the plains. The mountains never quit screaming at those of us who are a little deaf.

And the whole time the mountains have been screaming, the prairies have been singing, reluctant to press their demands in any bolder way. Some of us have treated the song as a lullaby. We didn't listen; we fell asleep.

A hundred years ago a group of speculators and developers got the idea that they could irrigate the land east of the Bighorn Mountains by diverting water from the slopes onto the flats. Miles of irrigation ditches were dug. Water never filled these ditches. Today there are still tracings of the ditches left on the land that rolls away to the south of Trabing Road and east of the Bighorns.

John and I continued pedaling east. We stared at the worn indentations that were to have been ditches. They were like huge neon signs blinking the fantasy and the failure of those who came here with grand schemes of transforming the land. John commented on how inviting the grass on the Colorado Flats looks. There's almost no sage or greasewood. Just miles of grass.

"Yup, looks good, all right," John said and told me he imagined hundreds of cows standing contentedly along the road. As we rode on, John said the cows shrank and became bands of sheep—hundreds and thousands of sheep standing and, like the cows, chewing. The horizontal slits of their eyes were dark windows onto unknown worlds. John smiled as he related this tale—the mirage of a cold, arid northern country.

The reality is that it would take only a few cows or sheep grazing here on the Flats to irrevocably stun the earth, which would then rise and flee in great gaseous clouds of dust. It's better for everyone concerned to head farther east to the ratty looking scrub desert which can better stand to be chewed on before it begins to blow away.

Once I was caught after dark bicycling home from Kaycee, forty-six miles to the south of Buffalo. The Bighorns rose to the west, while to the east the land sloped gently away, as it does here, seemingly forever. As the sun set, I turned my eyes away from the glare, and out onto open prairie. When the moon rose, the wind came up. I lifted my head and breathed deeply, sure that I could smell the ocean, hear its slap against the shore. Tired and slightly dizzy from riding in the dark, I was hypnotized and felt I should turn the bike off the road and into the great sea of sage which smelled impossibly of kelp.

I often require a sharp blow in order to awaken to what's around me.

There's a spot I know in the Bighorns where the water flows under a massive boulder field. You can hear the rumble and stir of water but you never see it. When I hike up this boulder field, I stop periodically to listen. Sometimes I throw myself face down on a large rock and press my ear to the cold surface. There is a hum and vibration of the nearby invisible water.

The poets Lew Welch and Gary Snyder were once out hiking in the mountains. After climbing for a long while, they sat down to rest. Welch said to Snyder, "Gary, what do you think the mountains think of the trees?"

Snyder looked at Welch and said, "What are you talking about, Lew?"

"Well, I was just thinking that to the mountains the trees are just passing through."

To see the spectacular, it is sufficient to remove the marks of human activity—the roads and buildings, wires and bridges—and the land opens before us, spectacular even if, in some cases, slightly shy. Maybe my slow coming to this feeling is what Rawlins meant when he wrote that our change can occur in unspectacular country, out of a will to know something besides ourselves.

When the first settlers came into northeastern Wyoming, they realized quickly that it was an arid land not suitable for the kind of farming that could be done in Iowa and Illinois. Land developers and immigrant agents then came up with a phrase that must be one of the great marketing scams of all time. The phrase was "Rain follows the plow." It would suffice, the promoters claimed, to break the earth and turn it. Shortly following this act, the clouds would begin to pile up and rain would fall, turning Wyoming into the rich farming state it was destined to be.

Certain people got rich while immigrant farmers learned that the only thing that truly follows the plow is the plowman.

After the Colorado Flats, the Trabing Road begins to undulate wildly up and down. John and I crouched over the handlebars of our bikes getting all the speed we could as we flew downhill. At the bottom of each hill, we threw ourselves into the climb, coasting as far as we could up then pedaling furiously to make the top of each hill before losing momentum. It was crucial that we judge the exactly correct moments to quit pedaling on the down slope and then to begin again on the up slope. A miscalculation would mean wasted effort and slower speed.

I was thinking in this manner as we rode then I looked around and thought, what am I talking about? Wasted effort? What are we measuring here? After that, at least for a brief time, I simply rode.

We followed the paved road toward Irigaray, then toward Malapai, the abandoned uranium mine. After about twenty miles of riding, we rose again with the road as it went through a long curve to the north. We were still on pavement but it would soon end. At the top of the curve the pavement doubled back to the east. We stopped at the topmost point and lay the bikes down.

I've always loved this act of setting a bicycle down on the ground, putting the machine in contact with the earth, encouraging the two to embrace. If any machine is capable of embracing the earth, it is the bicycle. Two strange distant cousins, falling in love.

We ate lunch. The sky was dark, the clouds boiling. It had gotten colder since we'd started. I looked at John. He ravenously wolfed down the sandwich, dried fruit and nuts we'd brought. We weren't carrying much food, as we'd expected to be at the ranch in a few hours. I could see that I'd miscalculated when I'd decided what to bring for the day. I was hungry and John seemed to be more so.

"Let's focus on supper," I said to John. We both knew that Margo would be driving out to Four Mile after she finished work in the pottery studio. She'd come into the ranch on the shorter route from the north, meet us at the cabin and the three of us would cook a huge meal.

John looked at me without speaking. Dinner was hours of effort away. For the moment we had two apples, a small sack of granola, another small sack of dried apricots and two quarts of water to last the rest of the ride.

John is from the Carolinas. To him Wyoming remains an appealing and slightly threatening expanse, an enigma. He is a kayaker, forced by circumstance here with me into riding a bicycle. Depending on which census you look at he is descended from Cherokee people, blacks, or whites. He looks like all of them. We've known each other for most of our adult lives and I'm happy to be here with him.

I've heard it said that solitude is our truest friend, that all other friendships erode, that only the hard rock under our feet will last. When I look at John I realize that this is not true. In nature, it is rock that erodes. However slowly, rock erodes and one day becomes sand, and then, in its marriage with living matter, becomes soil. Rock cannot help but erode. Friendship does not erode. Friendship in its momentariness can be infinite. It can be held onto no matter our losses or sorrows. The moment of friendship is eternity.

John and I stopped again, ostensibly to stare for a last

few moments at the ever more distant mountains. Really, we had stopped to rest. We knew this by the way we grinned at one another. When we began to ride again, it was slowly, gently working out the stiffness the stop had brought to our legs.

In a later part of his book, Rawlins says, "If living out here plunges us into a bodily closeness, it also makes us aware of the profound barriers between any two human selves." Like Rawlins, I have felt these barriers. The feeling has made me very sad. Now I believe the barriers were of my own making. The boundary between self and other has blurred. And as that boundary has blurred, I have felt more alive, more myself, more wedded to the earth and to its creatures, including my human companions.

During the year that she was five, my daughter Caitlin spent a lot of time drawing her hands. She'd set one hand down on a piece of paper and trace around it with a pencil held in her other hand. Then she'd switch and do the other hand. Often she would draw a face on one or more of the fingers. One such face had long dark hair— disheveled, spilling happily onto the fingers on either side. The face's eyes were wide open giving the end of the finger a wild, innocent, inquisitive look. The mouth was huge with great red lips.

Caitlin often gives me her drawings as little gifts. "For Dad" she writes on them. I have a folder filled with drawings that for one reason or another have meant a lot to me. I have numerous hands.

When I ride, or when I sit down to write of how life surprises, troubles and pleases me, or when I repair a windmill, or when I bring the horses into the corral to saddle them for work, my daughter's hands are with me.

At Camino's ranch, John and I headed northwest on the

rutted dirt road. We clattered down a dusty incline and into a series of gullies leading around an old shearing yard, a hired man's cabin, a defunct windmill and an empty pond. Shortly past the cabin we left the single track and began to ride on the sheep trails. Now the riding became truly difficult. We wound through sage, rabbitbrush, and greasewood then climbed a long ridgeline into open space. We passed through about a hundred cows bunched up on a piece of bare ground above a creek bed. We dropped into the creek bed and climbed out on the other side going northeast.

We could have ridden straight downstream with the creek and eventually would have come out on one of the western boundaries of Four Mile. Instead we headed cross country leaving even the sheep trails behind.

The going got harder still and, though I knew we were generally heading the right way, you could say we were lost. I mean we didn't know exactly where we were. Then off to the south there was a glint of light.

"Look, John, that glare is the roof of the shearing shed near Falxa's."

John turned and held his hand up to shield his eyes from the light.

The general fall of the land and the sun's path in the sky and, of course, the shed which is southwest of the southern entry to Four Mile all said we were moving northeast.

"Four Mile's big, John, we're bound to hit some edge of it." John remained unconvinced and I, too, felt some alarm.

After a long climb up one ridgeline, around a couple of scarred buttes, over a field of powdery dirt blackened by iron, we came to another ridgeline. It looked much like the last one. In every direction, for thousands of square miles, the ridges rose and fell with stunning similarity.

At the end of the next ridgeline we found ourselves staring over the edge of a cliff.

"Jump?" I said to John.

After a long silence in which we listened to the roll of the wind across the earth, John said only, "I can't pedal much farther. My thighs feel like spaghetti."

"Let's eat." I suggested, handing him the dried fruit and water. I suspect I was at least as tired as he was but I didn't care as much. Anyway, I couldn't care—I was the guide. "After we've eaten, we'll head back down and work our way around."

As we sat, I thought of the new colt Boomerang. He'd spooked while getting in the trailer, fallen over backwards and caught his hind legs under the sill. The right leg was badly torn up. It was in a plastic cast for two and a half months. Screwed up his gait. Now when he runs, instead of moving his right leg forward, he throws it out sideways in a little circle. Because of this, he puts more weight on his left front foot with each stride. It looks like he drops his left shoulder slightly with each footfall. But he runs full bore anyway as if nothing had happened. He has no hesitation. That's the way I want to keep going.

John was growing increasingly annoyed at me for getting us lost and then for being so perky about our condition. I was supposed to know where I was going. These ridges and gullies and washes and ravines and mica fields and gumbo pits and greasewood clusters and lines of cottonwood in the distance were replicating themselves faster than we could keep up.

I have lots of experience on a bike and I've spent a lot of time in this country. Still, if I move a hundred yards from my accustomed path everything is different while appearing the same.

When I accuse my wife Margo of losing something, she tells me sweetly, "It's not lost. I just don't know where it is."

Because John was getting truly worried and because I, too, was feeling a little anxious, I took off back down the ridgeline with John following and pedaled as rapidly as I could in the general direction I thought we should go. The ache in my thighs felt good. After not too many miles, I came down along a fenceline. Ah, a Four Mile boundary. I lifted the bike over the fence then, again, pedaled hard, bouncing furiously down the hillside to just above the creek bottom.

Before me was the junction of two trails. I recognized both. One led to the Traud windmill, the other to the South Pasture West windmill. As I had earlier, I laid the bike on the ground. I eased myself down next to it, lying flat on my back, looking around for the stubby cactus that is ubiquitous on the ranch. After disappearing into dark clouds, the sun had returned and the late afternoon light was warm. I was thirsty but we were almost out of water. I could wait till we got to a windmill or the cabin before I drank.

John came coasting down the hill looking quite distressed. He had his feet off the pedals and was dragging his toes—both to slow down and for balance.

"We're here," I chirped. "This is Four Mile."

John looked around and slowly began to grin. It was the same land he had been frowning at a moment ago. We were both relieved.

Rawlins says that "density of language often depends on a sparsity of experience." That phrase hit me as I lay there staring first at the nearby sky, then away toward the distant Traud mill which I knew to be down near the cottonwoods on the watercourse.

Sometimes I feel it isn't the paucity but the plethora of experience that hinders us. We have an experience and consequently think we know something. The truth is that there is only one thing stopping us from learning. It's knowledge. I'd like to come at each moment as if it were brand new, shimmering, alluring and, though I don't like being scared, a little scary. The moment never before seen. No experience.

We found a ranch road and went the rest of the way on the marked track. At the South Pasture West windmill, we found Simon hard at it with the backhoe. He was moving earth to stabilize the tower and to rebuild the shoreline of the pond. At every stock pond, the cows walk into the water and tear up the earth at the pond's edge, causing erosion and filling in of the reservoir. A good pond should be small in circumference and deep to minimize water loss through evaporation. A wider, shallower pond will hold as much water as a narrower deeper one, but the shallow wide pond loses more water to wind and sun.

Over time all windmill ponds grow shallower and wider. Cows devote much of their attention to helping that process along. No matter what you do to protect a pond, a windmill or a stock tank, cows will blunder into that protection and destroy it.

We got off the bikes and started working with Simon, shoveling by hand where the backhoe was too cumbersome to work. I was exhausted but felt happy shoveling, one shovelful after another, so that as my shoulders and back got sore I forgot the ache in my thighs.

Rancher

◆

f I love this work so much—life among the windmills and the cows, the space, the blisteringly hot summers and penetratingly cold winters, the ranch—why am I not a rancher? Why am I nothing more than my father-in-law's part-time ranch hand? I'm a good hand but no more. I talk and talk about the windmills and wonder if there comes a time when a person has to put up or shut up. Or, as my friends say nowadays, "walk the talk."

It's true I love the work. By "love it," I mean that it has saved my life. It has taken me outside both literally and figuratively. It has allowed me to have contact with my wife's family and with the community in which I live that I could not otherwise have had. It has helped me to live life on this earth rather than in some fantastic land that exists only inside my head. It has demanded that I pay attention to what is going on outside me, to become an observer. I've come to know the weather, the seasons, the grasses, the flow of wild and domestic animals—pronghorns, deer, coyotes, bobcats, cows, sheep—across the land.

Before I began working on the ranch, I thought I was supposed to judge everything. The ranch has helped me to move away from judging, and toward experiencing life as it is. This is very different from life as I imagined I wished it to be.

We are told that on the Day of Atonement, God will only be able to forgive those sins we have committed in the realm of ritual. That is, if we have failed to keep to the rituals, we can be forgiven for this failure. But we will not be absolved of our sins against other human beings, for we can atone for these sins only by redressing the wrong in this life. Each one of us must do this alone, and it will be impossible to do it after our deaths.

We must redress not only our sins against other human beings, but our sins against the plants and animals, the damage we do to the earth itself.

Having said that, I see that the things of the earth forgive us before we know we have committed a crime. They do not judge us. Nothing more is demanded of us than to go on, to live. Water neither judges us for leaving it imprisoned under the earth, nor for spilling it carelessly onto the dust into which it disappears.

I both love and fear seeing my life become one that is distant from "civilization." I long to be like the prairie dogs, the elk, the mountain lions, the eagles. I look fondly on the loathsome coyotes, the choking dust, the ill-tempered badgers, the dirty thieving raccoons, the dangerous rattlers.

My fondness for these last useless or destructive things is proof, according to some, that I'm no rancher. But I've met old-timers who love the varmints more than their own sheep and cows.

I must ask myself again: if I truly love this ranch life, why am I not a rancher? Why do I not give myself completely to ranching and to the land? Why do I stay in town? Why do I think it's important that I write down my thoughts and ideas?

My father was a laboring man. Until I was sixteen, he never had a regular job. He worked as a gardener, carpenter, handyman, assembly line "operative," janitor, maintenance man and painter. When he was at home, his hobbies were constructed from the same materials—he refinished furniture, tended iris and roses, built extra rooms on our house.

Watching my father, I learned that physical labor is right and true. It's what identifies a human being. When I am gardening (call it ranching) or building (call it windmill maintenance), I am alive in a way my father taught me. I am engaged. When I return to ordinary life, I smile, realizing my oblivion has been that of engagement.

My father showed me how to work but when he talked, his words carried another message. From as early as I can remember he told me that I was smart. What he meant by smart was that I would not have to be a working man. "A stumblebum like me," he said. That's what he called himself—a stumblebum.

I would not have to do physical labor. I would not come home so exhausted I could barely throw my head under the faucet for a drink of water before collapsing in a heap in the nearest chair. I would not spend weeks in a hospital then months at home doing nothing while my arms, crushed at work when a trailer fell on me, healed. I would not see again and again the trailer plunging toward me. I would not be driven crazy working in a steel shed, 112 degrees, sawdust in my hair and down my neck, mixing with my own sweat and making my skin raw. I would not lie in front of a television seeking oblivion, sleeping as the pictures whirled before me. I would not die in an alley in a burning city, my arms and legs purpled and swollen, my body temperature 109 degrees.

"Your life will be better than mine," my father told me. "You won't be out there breaking your back to survive."

The common fury that my father directed at me nearly always arose from his bitterness following some action of mine that was not the "smart" thing. For years, my father could only look sadly at me and say, "Brains to burn and you can't earn a goddamned living." But when I was a child, he thought that my brains would mean I'd never have to be a slave to some other man.

He taught me to work and he taught me that work was somehow demeaning. He showed me his struggle for meaning through his work and he told me that I was better than working people.

"You are better than me," he said, and "You're an idiot."

The confusion—or perhaps collision—shows up in my adult life. I love both my work with windmills and my work as a writer. Just as I do not repair a windmill only to watch the water rise from the earth, neither do I write only to tell you what I think.

The spinning blades of the windmill are the motors of a rocket lifting off and flying to distant planets. The word "palpable" is as tangible as the windmill itself. The physical chores I do as a ranch hand become the images in my writing, while the abstractions I make as a writer are as solid as the stones and soil of Four Mile.

In my inability to give myself wholly to one or the other

of my labors, I give myself to both. Sometimes I am so exhausted by work on the ranch that when night comes I cannot hold my eyelids open. On these nights, I sit at my desk and try to write while my wife and daughter sleep. My vision blurs and my head slowly falls forward onto the computer keyboard. I land nose first and there is a whirring from the hard drive as ten or fifteen keys go down at once. Then the whirring stops. The house is still. I rise and go to bed.

As I am engaged when working on a windmill, so I am engaged finding my way inside words. The world falls away and there are only dark images on a smooth surface. The word is not a description of the world; it is the world.

There is one last reason why I am not a full-time rancher. It arises from the shame my father gave me about physical labor, but it is not this shame. It is more insidious. In my moments of despair at the meaninglessness of life, I imagine that worldly fame is the answer. A famous person is respected and admired by all and so has a life of meaning. Who ever heard of a famous windmill worker? So I'll be a writer. My books will sell hundreds of thousands of copies and I'll make plenty of money. People will tell me that I am good, witty, intelligent, thoughtful, incisive, that my work opens the reader to the transcendent possibilities of life.

This is all bullshit, but I am learning to smile about it, to forgive myself, and to keep writing. Just as the ranch teaches me to stop judging others, it helps me to stop judging myself.

Once on a winter day—a very cold winter day—I needed to find our horses—Trouble, Penelope (also known as P-Brain), Harold, Bobo, Fergie, Cinnamon. I thought they were in the Bridge Pasture—the pasture where we'd just put in another electric mill. I grabbed a halter and a partially full bag of oats and began to walk up and down the ridgelines, looking as far as I could down the draws on both sides. Walking rapidly, sometimes running, I was aware that the horses can always stay one ridge ahead of me. By running I thought I might catch them. Running kept me warmer, too.

I moved down into the cottonwoods along the watercourse. Stepping through the trees, I could hear the bare branches creaking and snapping in the wind. My face was raw. The bag of oats was heavy. The halter line kept falling off my shoulder and getting tangled around my legs. I went up the other side of the creek bed and walked the ridgelines in the north half of the pasture.

I whistled for the horses, but my lips were frozen so that the whistle was no more than a tiny thin whisper of breath. I had to take a glove off to put my fingers in my mouth and make a loud whistle. A couple of seconds exposed and the fingers felt as if they would crack off and splinter into many small pieces.

"Trouble, P-Brain, Harold. Hey, hey, horses, come on you horses." I have sought these horses for years now and I can picture them lifting their heads when they hear me calling. They listen for a moment, then put their heads back down to the earth. They paw through the snow to get at the frozen grass. They eat the snow to get water.

A few years after I moved to Wyoming, my father visited. During his visit, he pulled me aside and whispered in my ear, "How long are you going to stay in this godforsaken place?"

I told him, "You know I've got all this education, I've been trained to be some kind of head worker and yet the two things you taught me that I love above all else are gardening and carpentry. They're connected to ranching and to my staying here. You gave me that."

My father seemed disappointed.

When I began writing, my father tried his best to stop me— "How you gonna make a living at that?" As he read my poems, his face darkened. He'd go from being confused to angry to outraged. "Goddammit, this makes no sense. What's a person supposed to do with this? Who'd want to read something that nobody in his right mind could understand?"

It was as though I was trying to put something over on him.

When I published my first poem, my father borrowed the literary magazine in which the poem appeared and took it to work. He showed it to the men who worked with him in the maintenance department for the county.

"This is my son," he said. "He's a published poet."

Life is not what we label it, nor is it synonymous with its identifying features. There is a way for us to be writers and ranchers both—clowns and horticulturists, physicists and evangelical ministers, U.S. senators and blackjack dealers, alcoholics and oceanographers.

At the ranch the cows saunter up to the stock tank, drawn by any human working there, assured that soon the flow of water will begin again. Not one cow keeps track of the number stamped on her ear tag. The birds fly overhead. Some of them are banded, and so they too have the opportunity to ignore their numbers. The prairie dogs whistle and chirp then disappear into their underground homes. When they eat poison oats, they die. More prairie dogs are born.

Underground, the water is neither silent nor still. It

flows in dark rivers and rests in dark lakes. It is rocked by the continuous turning of the earth. There are tides in the water below us, the waves rolling, the water pressing against the shores then receding.

One day working on the Gas Plant windmill I slipped while descending the tower for a tool I'd forgotten. I grabbed the ladder and hung there for a moment with my feet waving around in space. When I got my feet back on the rung, my head was spinning and I realized that I had been given the opportunity to fly.

Winter Walk

♦

One January day I set off walking from Buffalo to Story along the face of the Bighorn Mountains. It had been fiercely cold and so there was little work that I could do at Four Mile. The cattle had been shipped in the fall and there would be no stock on the ranch until spring. I'd been trying to get out to the ranch to check on the horses fairly often, taking a little alfalfa and barley cake and walking slowly in the Bridge Pasture until I stumbled onto them. They'd eat what I brought, and I'd talk to them for a while. When they'd finished eating, they would watch me for several minutes then wander away, usually to the northwest. I'd walk back to the cabin.

The horses were always fine and would have been fine whether I'd come or not. I just wanted to see them and see the land in winter, a time of both dramatic violence and somnolence. Either way the days move with glacial slowness. The sun's up late and down early. I sleep a lot, feeling about like that old gentleman who wondered if he was a man dreaming that he was a butterfly or a butterfly dreaming that it was a man.

One morning when I woke it was fifteen degrees—a little warmer than it had been. I wanted to get out and do something and I wanted it to be physically demanding. So I decided I'd walk to Story. When I got there, I would spend the night at a friend's house, and the friend would drive me back to Buffalo the next morning.

It's about twenty-two miles to Story—as the crow flies. But in the end the walk turned out to be somewhat longer than the flight of that crow. Several times I had to detour around drifted snow or icy bogs. I also got lost a few times and, once, I decided to walk in the wrong direction because I liked the look of a small stand of aspen that I would otherwise not pass through.

Aside from these deviations I tried to follow as directly as I could the line of the mountains. This meant that I sometimes walked along a road and sometimes cut cross-country.

I left Buffalo at 8:30 in the morning. The sky was dark. I wore long underwear, navy wool pants and a brown wool shirt, a scarf, jacket, headband and hat, gloves, wool socks and a pair of old hiking boots—fifteen-year-old comfortable boots. In my pack I carried water, dried fruit, nuts, two sandwiches of cheese, tomato and green pepper, an extra pair of shoes and socks. For January, it wasn't particularly cold, and dressed as I was, I felt warm.

I also felt happy, a spinning crazy dizzy vertigo of happiness as if I'd been struck in my sleep by just the right kind of lightning. I often feel this way in winter—something about sun and ice, or silence and wind. And it's comforting to get away from town, away from buildings and roads and electric wires. What would happen if I were away from these forever? I cannot say. I like to think it would be heaven but I'm not so sure and think it presumptuous to imagine my reaction. For now, the escape is glorious. Town fades behind me and the part of life that seems dark and bitter fades, too.

Some things do not fade. As I walked I couldn't stop myself from noticing beer cans along the road, the roar of chain saws and hum of distant airplanes, the dark strip of pavement unrolling before me. I got mad and thought, "We are sucking the juices out of our planet as if we could keep sucking until it was a dead dry husk which then we'd throw on the garbage heap."

Then I walked again, wondering what good anger ever did me, or my encumbered planet.

I daydreamed about a novel I read. The main character is a Lakota woman who has married a white man. The husband regularly beats up his wife. He blackens her eyes. Twice he cut her with a knife and once he broke her left wrist when he grabbed her. The woman finally ran away, vowing she would never again marry a white man.

She could just as well have blamed the beatings on the fact that she'd married a man and vowed that next time she'd marry a woman. Or she could have seen the root of the problem in marriage and simply promised never to sign that contract again.

It made me think of how we label one another. Some white person says, "Oh, yes, he's my Arapaho friend" or "She's a fine black writer."

Odd. I wonder if there is a novel in which the main character is a sage grouse or a bit of greasewood. That would be good—a greasewood bush for a hero or heroine. Its only method of speaking would be through the animals that eat it.

The sky was gray. Actually, it would be better to say "grays." There are more shades of gray than all the drops of rain that have ever fallen. Where there was no snow, the earth was brown, and the grasses golden—yellow, cornflower, amber, straw.

I climbed fences to cross fields. Even in this land which people feel is so wide and open, there are fences everywhere. A few years ago, two friends of mine rode their horses from the Mexican border near Douglas in southern Arizona to the Canadian border in Glacier Park, Montana. "We opened and closed over 450 gates on that ride," they told me. "One time, after a long day's ride up a river and a wild scramble down steep cliffs, we camped far up a canyon. It looked like no one had been there for a long time. At three in the morning, we were rousted by a forest ranger."

"What happened?" I asked.

"He said to move along. Get out, you know. 'Jesus, it's three in the morning,' we told him, like maybe he didn't know that. 'We'll be up and out of here first thing the sun comes up.' And the ranger said, 'No, you'll be up and out of here now. No camping and no horses allowed.' And he stood there while we packed the gear, loaded the horses and moved."

It made me think of the times I've been out on long bike trips. I stop and before pulling off the road look around to make sure no one sees me. I find a hidden spot and set up my tent. If the weather's good, or if it looks as if I might get rousted, I simply roll out a sleeping bag.

All over the United States, I've had to go into hiding in order to camp. I've searched out the deepest woods, the darkest most out-of-the-way spots. Always hiding—from the landowner, from a park ranger, from county sheriffs, from forest service officials. What an idea it is that in this vast huge country it is often necessary to hide in order to sleep outside on the ground.

The average human population density for the earth is now 85 people per square mile. For Wyoming the figure is about 4.6 people per square mile. To me, the Wyoming figure is high.

On one bike trip I was riding across southeastern Arizona. There were no woods. The land was nearly flat and open with stands of saguaro fading into great expanses of creosote. After a long day of pedaling, and far from any town or ranch, I came upon a cemetery. Though there were a few new graves here and there, it was an old cemetery with eroded and crooked headstones rising from bare ground. In the back of the cemetery there was a stand of mesquite trees. Exhausted, I rode in, got off my bike and wheeled it into the mesquite.

It was as though I had entered a crackling dry grotto. The grass was beaten down as if someone had prepared a bed for me. I drank a little water and then, without eating, fell asleep.

I awoke to a brilliant light shining in my face and two men demanding to see my identification. They were policemen. They were harsh, threatening to take me in, to handcuff me, all the time shining the light in my eyes so that it was hard to see them.

"How did you find me?" I asked.

"We were patrolling and as we rounded the curve here at the back of the cemetery there was a flash in the trees. We turned and there it was again so we came looking."

"The reflector on my bike," I said. "I'll have to remember to cover it." The cops almost smiled. They were beginning to see that I was only what I appeared to be, a sleeping bicyclist.

"We've had a lot of trouble out here. There's a group of local people, I don't know, Rumanian or something Eastern European. These people bury valuables with their deceased. Rings and necklaces, you know, really valuable stuff—diamonds and gold. We find graves dug up pretty regular, coffins opened and ransacked. Sometimes the grave robbers just toss the body out on the ground and leave it. You wouldn't believe it. We thought we'd caught a grave robber."

"Me?"

"Yeah, you."

Then we got to talking—there in the tiny mesquite grove, in the warm desert night, the two cops sitting cross-legged on the ground. They wanted to know all about my ride—where I'd come from, where I was going.

"Boy, I'd like to do something like that sometime," one said, handing me back my driver's license.

"It's nice," I said. "You see a lot."

"You remember to cover up that reflector," they laughed, as they got back in the patrol car. "Be careful." I waved as they drove off then went back to sleep. The stars were smiling down at me.

I woke from my daydream of a past bike trip. I was about five miles out of Buffalo, staring down at a mirror torn off the side of a pickup. I picked the mirror up to look at my reflection. But the glass had long since been broken out and I saw nothing in the rusty surface.

"I don't exist!" I cried and dropped the mirror. "Ha-ha! Only joking."

Thinking of various Zen Buddhist pranks, I reared back and threw the empty mirror as far away as I could. Some antelope will look down into it, see the rusty reflection of a human being and bolt.

A little later I came upon fresh scat. I bent over to look at it, trying to figure out if it was deer or antelope. Behind the hillock formed when the road builders leveled the grade was a circle of matted grass—a deer bedding ground. At first I thought that this meant that the scat, too, must belong to deer. Then I realized there was no necessary connection between the two. I knew no more than before.

I stopped walking in order to feel the silence. It was a kind of silky thick silence that could be held and caressed, a delicious smooth singing silence. Sonic booms, diesel engines, irrigation pumps—each one making noise but they all wear out or break or give up and when they do, the silence sings again.

Now beside the road, there were old livestock auction posters and notices of foreclosure sales, blown tires, a still usable boot, aluminum foil, an empty margarine tub, a half-full can of motor oil, rusted barbed wire, fiberglass insulation, unidentifiable pieces of styrofoam, cans, bottles, paper, plastic bags, a dollar bill, a five dollar bill, the grill of a car, the door of a car, the bumper of a car, the muffler of a car, survey stakes, a length of concrete pipe, ropes and ribbons.

If I were stranded here alone, if the world as I know it had come to an end and if I were the last person alive, I could begin again the same civilization I had so recently left behind by collecting what had been tossed away by those who preceded me.

Thoreau asked, "What is a course of history or philosophy, or poetry, no matter how well selected, or the best society, or the most admirable routine of life, compared with the discipline of looking always at what is to be seen?" I wondered. Then Thoreau said, "Read your fate, see what is before you, and walk on into futurity."

But I could not. Thoreau said he had gone into the woods when it was time for that, and, later, he had returned to civilization when it was time for that. Walking, I had neither fully left civilization nor fully accepted it. I had been swept along by a torrent of worn-out, unloved, abandoned products cascading from factories and stores as if there would be no end.

As I walked farther from town, the thrown-away things sank deeper into the grass. Even in Wyoming, where the wagon ruts from a hundred years ago remain visible, the grass will one day completely cover the metal and plastic and paper thrown in its midst.

I could hear water running far away, muffled by winter's ice and snow. The cottonwoods were bare and twisted, writhing in agony, maybe, or dancing like mad happy children.

As I came up a long hill, a black cloud rose toward me and yet the Bighorns remained bathed in sunlight. There was a huge mound of horse droppings, busily turning into golden stones.

I stepped around a silent sheepdog, dead and beginning to bloat. Even in death the dog seemed tense and ready, still a living part of this world. As she had in life, she waited patiently in death. No longer called upon to move sheep, the dog willingly began to turn back into what she had been before—the grasses and trees, the eagles and hawks, her bad-boy cousin Coyote, the wind.

Going on I passed more dead animals, both the dead by

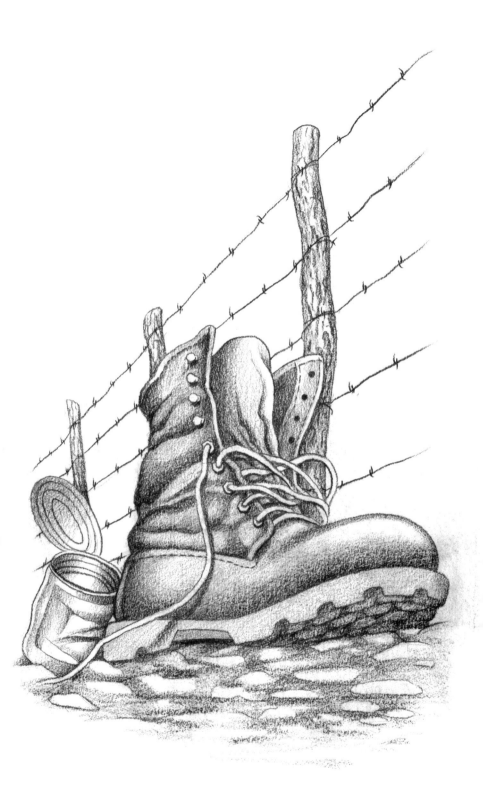

the side of the road and those left in the fields. Of a deer there remained only a tangle of legs shedding fur and skin, the bones still connected in spots by cartilage that was shiny and smooth. There was a dead pronghorn, a dead house cat, a dead rabbit, each growing quickly less recognizable to me and more like its silent neighbors.

I came over a hillside to a ravine filled with abandoned cars. Some lay upside down, some on their sides, some right side up and ready to be driven away. A Ford Galaxy from the mid-sixties settled into the earth—wheels gone, doors, trunk and hood removed.

There were dumps everywhere. Inside the dumps were smaller specialty dumps. I felt a temptation to wander among the long corridors of garbage, hoping I'd find some forgotten but still useful item.

As I climbed a fence to leave the road again, I noticed coils of hair tangled up in the barbed wire—the spot where the cows had rubbed themselves. There was a tire buried in ice, a sheen of melt water over a black ring. The magpies called, the wind picked up out of the northwest. A muffler had fallen from a car and somehow ended here, far from the road along which the car had passed. A flock of geese flew overhead. The smell of sage enveloped me.

Just walking, one foot in front of another, one foot after another. That's how nature does it. Consider the plants, how they release their seeds which fly in the wind, or are carried by animals. Then the seeds drop on this dry ground and try to sprout. Millions of seeds and maybe one or two take root and grow.

Six feet away a group of birds leapt from the brush with a frantic drumlike beating of wings. I leapt back. Each of us was frightened by the sudden presence of the other. My heart thumped fiercely in my chest. They were some kind of gallinaceous bird, partridge or quail or chukar, that men hunt— henlike, heavy-bodied birds who imagine they can survive by staying hidden until the last possible moment. Only if nearly stepped on will they flee, crashing furiously away from whatever threatens them by its approach. There were eight birds.

A winter rabbit, brilliantly white, rose from another bush a step away from me. I could see the rabbit's dilated pupils as it fled. I followed a watercourse, then an empty irrigation ditch. Finally I was walking through sage again.

Far out in the country, I returned to the road. The pavement had ended and the road was a single dirt track which passed only scattered homesteads. Mounted atop a creosoted log far from its house was a lone mailbox. Painted on the mailbox were a rainbow and the words, "Smile, God loves you."

Then the road was gone for good. I walked up and down hills, crossing ridgelines, moving deep into wet, cold draws, down into dark shadow and back up again into light. In some places there was deep drifted snow, in others the ground was bare, swept by wind and sun.

A bald eagle rested at the top of a cottonwood. I turned my head away and in the moment it took me to turn back the eagle had lifted and was two hundred yards away. I followed its motion then, for no reason I know, turned to look over my right shoulder. Far up a ridgeline standing on a boulder was a second eagle looking down, not at me so much as through me.

Between the two eagles was a band of pronghorn— maybe forty or fifty. They moved too fast and too close together to be counted. They ran the way a flock of birds flies. The pronghorn surged forward and back, side to side. They turned, hesitated, turned again and ran on. And like the birds, they moved as if they were one creature with flexible skin, their outer boundary fluid and permeable.

I couldn't say exactly where I was and so stayed close to the foothills, walking northwest with the mountain range. For a long time I followed a fenceline. Eleven horses ran toward me, pushing to smell me. They shoved each other and the fence. They nipped at my coat, looking for the gift I must have brought—oats, maybe, or corn. Sadly, I had no gift. I climbed the fence and stood with the horses. I picked one out and stayed with him a long time. I lay down in the field, in a dry spot between patches of snow, and closed my eyes. When I stood I rubbed the horse down with my hands, scratching his face, ears, nose, using my fingers like a brush. For many days after, my wool gloves would carry the smell of a horse I didn't know.

As the horses ran toward me, a group of whitetail deer ran away from me, their great snowy puffs of tail flipping spasmodically left to right, then right to left.

I came down from the foothills and crossed a pasture near the town of Story. I walked quietly through a cluster of bulls, their dark coats dripping as they thawed, their strong breath rising in clouds from black nostrils. I crossed a creek and walked through another pasture, this one full of cows.

When I came out onto the road again, a hawk circled above me. It followed my movement for a long time then gave a parting call—a long bright wavering scream. I sighed and when I inhaled the air tasted different. I had been filled with sage for fifteen miles and now I smelled pine—raw, resiny and strong.

The other day I read the results of two polls taken in 1967 and 1987. The polltakers claimed that in 1967 two-thirds of the college students in the United States, when asked what was the most important thing about a job, said, "That the work be satisfying." In 1987 the same proportion of students—two-thirds—said, "The most important thing is money."

On the bare top of a hill I found the bones of another deer—an ordinary mule deer. The skull lay partially under the dirt, one eye socket aimed up to the sky. I picked the skull up and tugged and tugged at the teeth. I rocked them back and forth, side to side, up and down, until I broke them loose, one tooth at a time. I kept at it until I had ten teeth and I put them in my pocket where they would rattle, where I could feel them or take one out and hold it. Then I held the skull up, worked the jaw open and looked through. I looked at the ground and at the sky, looked at a cottonwood and a sage, and out toward the oncoming pines. It was exciting to look through the skull like this.

I thought I would walk from Buffalo to Story along the face of the Bighorns. A day long walk, in sun and shade, warmth and cold. I don't know what it was I thought I would gain, or learn, or what I would see that would be important. I don't know what idea I had about this walk. I wish I could say I had no idea at all, that I would only walk, one step after another. But I don't often possess this perfect richness and poverty of being.

I know it is dangerous to speak of happiness, but this walk, like my work on the windmills, made me happy. Happiness was what I gained, happiness which is a momentary reminder of something more that is much harder to name. A Zen teacher once said that happiness is not what enlightenment is about but that happiness must precede any chance of enlightenment. That makes me smile.

Parade

◆

County Fair and Rodeo Week in Buffalo, Wyoming. The arena is a mile from our house but we can hear the announcer's voice over the P.A. Around eleven at night, all the windows in the house open, Margo and I lie in bed and listen as the wind lifts the sounds of the rodeo and carries them to us.

It's impossible to make out the announcer's exact words but that doesn't matter. I know what's being said and I can hear the rodeo—bronc busting, bull riding, steer wrestling, calf roping, barrel racing. Barrel racing is my favorite and, truthfully, it's the only rodeo event I enjoy. All the others seem pure treachery and cruelty—both to man and beast.

Barrel racing, though, is a small communion for horse and rider—the horse's skill in that moment of explosive acceleration followed by severe braking to make the turn, the rider's skill in staying out of the horse's way, in using the weight and lean of her body to help the horse around the barrels.

Margo's favorite of our horses—Trouble—is an ex-barrel racer. Though he's seventeen years old, he's still the fiercest and the fastest of the horses at Four Mile. Now and again, when we have him in town, Margo will ride Trouble up Main Street to the fairgrounds so that he can run on the track, make a few fast turns. As he approaches the arena, he'll begin to breathe hard, flare his nostrils, and slap the ground with his feet.

Each night during rodeo week, after the events at the fairgrounds end, local kids and out-of-towners cruise Main Street, then cruise US 16 east. They idle languidly along Buffalo's tiny franchise row, stopping at Taco John's, A & W, Pizza Hut. They order bean and beef burritos, a Coke and fries, a pepperoni pizza. The ones who are old enough pull up to the drive-in window at Wa-Hoo Likkers. They order half cases of Bud Light and Coors. Deep into the night there is the honking of car horns and the shouting of hoarse voices. At first I hated this, now it feels warm and welcome. After winters as long as ours, nothing is better than to stay outside all day and all night, and for any reason, doing anything.

The Johnson County Fair and Rodeo Parade is Saturday morning at ten, same as forever. This year, Simon and I worked at the ranch every day of rodeo week. It seemed that all the windmills had broken down at once. The summer had been dry, hot and dusty. Every time we turned around there was a cow squalling at us for water. We'd replaced a lot of sticks, pulled entire wells to get to check valves and leathers, tried to straighten heads, repaired or replaced tanks.

Each night after work I went home exhausted. Driving back to Buffalo, I stared out the pickup window at the dark silhouette of the Bighorns and the chalky light of the moon.

During the week the moon went from less than half to gibbous, taking on a fat off-center look.

When Friday afternoon came, there were still repairs to be done but Simon and I both knew they'd have to wait. Saturday was the parade. We left the rig truck right where it was, backed up to the Traud mill, ready to go when we got back on Sunday.

In the last few years, there's been a pre-parade Saturday event—a ten kilometer run. The rodeo crowd and the runners don't mix much. Still, I don't think either group begrudges the other its time or its vision. And I, one of the runners, think the two groups share a great deal. Rodeo, after all, is the traditional work of Westerners made into play. And though it is more indirect, running is that, too. It makes the same demands on our bodies that traditionally have been placed upon us in order to survive—stamina, strength, will, the ability to endure a certain level of pain, the recognition that transcending this pain brings great pleasure and satisfaction. And in both rodeo and running we do it for no other reason than to do it.

The run begins with a long climb up Klondike Hill. At the top the road drops sharply, turns to dirt then climbs again, rising steadily until just after mile three. We run south along the Bighorn Range then turn west as if to run straight into the mountains. Another curve and we head east back to town, the last two miles gently downhill. We follow Clear Creek, cottonwoods lining the road, dappled shade on the earth. At 8:30 it's hot—Wyoming high country late summer hot. As I run under the cottonwoods' branches, I close my eyes to feel the sensation of light and dark on my eyelids. A little afraid I'll collide with another runner, I open my eyes, turn my head and look back at the Bighorns, the sunburnt mountains below a wide blue sky, the intensely white cumulus clouds.

This, to me, is the meaning of the West—the arid open space, mountains rising somewhere nearby, the mottled brown earth with only occasional green trees—stands of cottonwood and aspen along the watercourses, the road a gravel or dirt one-lane affair. It is the land I love and I'm sad to see it disappear under the weight of ranches and railroads and mines.

It is easy to be sad, though, and even on a developed stretch of highway, there is cause for joy. Black-eyed Susans and purple thistle approach the pavement. Below the asphalt, grasses grow, lifting the black smooth surface and cracking through it. Somebody has dropped a bale of hay and the smell of it slams into me as I run past, breathing heavily. From the weeds grasshoppers rise—they are hated for their destruction of our economies, but they are alive.

When the run ends, I hurry to South Main Street to line up for the parade. As the musical accompanist for the Bighorn Basque Dancers, I march every year in both the rodeo parade and in the Basque parade which usually takes place a few days later. For both parades, the dancers and I wear one of the village costumes of the northern Basque Provinces—white cotton pants and shirts for the men, red and black skirts with white blouses and black vests for the women. The men also wear black or red berets, red sashes, and red neckerchiefs. The women's hair is done up in long plaits. All of the dancers wear light soft cotton shoes. The dancers move down the street doing a traditional Basque parade dance. One part of the dance is straightforward marching, another includes some of the leaps that occur in

almost all Basque dances. So much of Basque dance happens in the air, as though the dancers might any minute take flight and disappear into the heavens.

I walk alongside the dancers playing the parade dance on a three-row button accordion—one of the instruments the Basque people brought with them when they left their homes in Euskadi for Wyoming. Behind the dancers is a pickup pulling a hay trailer decorated in red, white and green, the colors of the Basque national flag. And behind the trailer there are usually a few sheepwagons, including ours brought out from its exile in the backyard to remind us of its history and function. I love to see the sheepwagons rolling down the street with the name of the family they belong to taped to the canopy—Iberlin, Harriet, Marton and others.

I'm not Basque but because I've married into a Basque family I have become a kind of semiofficial backdoor Basque. As accompanist to the dance troupe, I'm proud to represent the Basque people. I am also proud to represent a part of our Western heritage that is often ignored amidst the romanticized media image of the West as only cowboys and Indians.

This year the Basque Dancers appeared at the very front of the parade and so when we finished I was able to stop and watch the rest of the parade pass. Much of it makes me uneasy and ashamed. It seems to honor the West of the Cowboys killing Indians, of the mountain men fleeing Europe without entering America, of the makers of manifest destiny eradicating or sending into exile entire peoples, of the voices of Christian evangelism denying other beliefs. It reminds me a little too clearly of my heritage as a white man, an interloper who came here to displace first the human beings whose culture my people scorned, later the animals who could never learn the bitter knowledge of our ways, and finally the very plants and earth, unwilling to voluntarily give themselves up to our ends.

Buffalo, Wyoming, is named not for the spirit and memory of a now nearly absent animal, but for a city in the state of New York. For me our town's name typifies the ambivalence I feel about my American past. On the one hand there is noise, laughter and camaraderie— this is a parade and it is for fun. On the other hand there is a whispered yet clear message about our history.

Near the front of the parade marches the Sheridan Drum and Bugle Corps. The men dress in the dark blue of Custer's Seventh Cavalry and carry the Seventh's banners. Though Custer and his troops were killed in 1876, they are resurrected each year for the parade. A drum major leads the troops. Between the drum major and the first row of men walk two young white women dressed as hip Eastern woodlands Indian maidens. Each woman wears a beige buckskin miniskirt and blouse. There is fringe around the hips and bust, accentuating shapely bodies. Each woman's hair is tied with feathers and beads. The women wear nylon stockings with their buckskins. These two women are the only representations of the Indian people in the Corps. They are the only representations of Indians in the parade.

When I put this together—the marching men, two beautiful young white women dressed as Indians, the banners of the Seventh Cavalry—I come face up to a large historical fact: the European rape of the North American continent. It is an old story and it has been told many times before. If I speak of it again—briefly—it is not to induce guilt but to ask myself what good may come of remembering.

Indian women were raped, brutalized and murdered. All Indian people were patronized and lied to, forcibly moved, cheated and, in the end, also murdered.

In the parade, the white race is presented as male, the Indian as female. Vine Deloria, Jr. tells the story that when he worked in a historical site visitor center, white tourists repeatedly told him they were part Indian. Deloria observed that almost all these white people claimed to be Indian through their grandmother or great-grandmother. They were all descended from Indian princesses.

In the front row of the Drum and Bugle Corps marches a man who looks to be in his mid-sixties. He's sweating, playing a snare drum with ferocity and, it appears, joy. He smiles, hops from left to right as he walks. It's hot and sweat rolls down his face, stains his dark blue uniform an even darker blue. He's loosened his neckerchief and opened his collar. All military order has broken down in him. He doesn't touch his pistol in its holster, he doesn't care about his uniform. It is the drumming that has captured him. I'll bet this is one of only a few times a year he gets to do this—be a performer, be a drummer, be a rhythm man on a hot day both for and with his friends and neighbors.

At first, I'm annoyed by the Seventh Cavalry reenactment and its implicit acceptance of what the real Seventh Cavalry did here in northern Wyoming and southeastern Montana. But then I look again at the drummer. Perhaps history has nothing to do with this drumming, with this man's experience. If this is true, then racial genocide has nothing to do with it. Hatred and fear of women has nothing to do with it. It's about drumming; it's about transcending the daily routine.

Here's a grand idea that now strikes me as very possible: all of this historical reenactment is really a way to deny the power of certain vivid and violent past events to hold us. This man's drumming is a voice that turns to the past and says, "No more. From now on, it won't be murder, it'll be drumming." So this man's drum carries a message for me that I can begin to see in the rest of the parade.

Here's a three-piece band on a trailer—a singer, guitarist and accordionist. They play country-western versions of Middle European polkas. On a banner behind the trailer is written "Heritage of Happiness."

And here are the marching cowboys. They walk, legs spread wide, boots and chaps and spurs, sweat-stained hats. They carry pistols, rifles, shotguns, and they fire all these guns randomly into the air. Sometimes they fire straight at each other and no one is hurt. They never fire into the crowd. The noise makes dogs bark and babies cry.

Now come the Shriners in Kalif outfits—the Kalif Hillbilly Band, Kalif Oriental band, the Kalif precision go-cart team.

Everyone in the county seems to be running for public office and the parade is a chance to campaign. Walking along the sidewalks, people pass out campaign literature. The candidates wave at potential voters. Many of the candidates throw candy to the crowd. I saw a preschooler get hit in the cheek with a piece of hard candy. The child cried for a minute then ate the candy.

Children from town and from the country walk along in costume. One's dressed as a gorilla and carries a sign reading, "I'm not the mayor's grandson." A whole group is dressed in cardboard boxes, faces painted on the backs of their heads. They are wrapped entirely in black plastic and shining aluminum foil. False arms dangle uselessly at their sides. One child's feet have been replaced with huge blocks of wood. Another is dressed in old newspapers, world events serving as a surrogate body. It's unclear what all this represents but the group makes me think of the mutant survivors of a nuclear war.

After the mutant group comes another children's group. They carry a banner that says "Back to the Future" and are all dressed alike in spotless snow-white jumpsuits. They walk silently, calmly, looking left to right. Their heads are encased in silver helmets. Because they follow the mutant group, they might be technicians cleaning up after the nuclear disaster.

A group of Senior Citizens rides by in a horse-drawn carriage. The Seniors do not wave to the crowd. No one in the crowd waves to the Seniors.

The Mountain Man club goes by—buckskin pants and jackets and fur hats. One man leads an eight-mule pack train. He's grizzled, tiny rivers of muddy sweat run down his face, he wears cracked dry leather, his spurs rattle against the pavement.

Behind the pack train come the Sheridan County Equestrianettes, women riding sidesaddle and wearing shiny aqua-blue skirts and blouses. Near the end of the parade walks a large overweight woman dressed in black stretch pants with silver piping. She leads two miniature horses—black steeds about waist high. People sigh and tell each other the little horses are cute. When one whinnies, its tiny voice high and ratchety, the crowd laughs and people say, "Oh, listen."

That's the parade. August in Buffalo, Wyoming. I try to

make sense of it all, the mysterious conjoining of elements I can't accurately name. The crowd laughs and I lean forward. There is a voice that whispers, addressing itself directly to me, and I can almost make out what's being said.

Machinery ♦

A s we were coming into Four Mile the other day, we met the pumper out blading the road. Though he works for the oil company that holds the federal leases on subsurface rights, he uses Simon's road grader to smooth the tracks into the oil wells. In return, he blades the Four Mile road, too. I don't like this system in which ranchers don't own what's under their land and I especially don't like the destruction of the landscape and the noise that goes along with the oil wells. Still, the pumper's a nice guy so it's hard to dislike him. He was glad to see us—asked if we'd move his pickup over to where he'd leave the grader when he finished blading.

It's a big Chevy pickup with airplane captain style seats—wraparound arms and a dashboard with a lot of lights and buttons. I grabbed the door handle, pulled while swinging up and nearly wrenched my arm off—the door was locked. This road is about as near to the middle of nowhere as a person could ever hope to find, and the pumper had his pickup locked.

"Hey, you trying to keep out curious coyotes?" I shouted, but he couldn't hear anything over the noise of the blading.

The windows were rolled up tight and the sun was blazing the way it does in September if it's not snowing. I unlocked the door. When I opened it, the trapped heat poured out. Right behind the heat came an overpowering sweet smell—pine-tree cardboard car deodorizers. Three hung from the mirror.

We left the pickup at the top of the hill and went down to Four Mile. Something about the bright newness of the Chevy, the intensity of the sweet artificial pine smell, the bare cleanliness of the cab, all made me think of machines.

At the ranch we're far from town working with cows or sheep or grass, but with machines, too. And I, as windmill technician, work constantly with machines.

The windmills themselves are machines. When they break it takes other machines to fix them. Once, working on the South Pasture Reservoir mill, everything that could go wrong did. It was a day of broken everything—sheared-off outlet pipe, threads embedded in other threads, two broken sticks and one had the bad manners to break not at the pipe joint but in the middle of two sections of pipe so it was a pain to get the stick out of the hole, a cracked galvanized coupling, the cast connector at the bottom of the pump rod split in half, leathers bashed, and a platform board that snapped off when I stepped on it so that I about did a nose dive for earth. It was tools and machines to correct the problems.

The biggest machines are the vehicles—the Ford pickup with the flatbed, the old gold Jeep pickup with the short wheelbase which makes it capable of going where the Ford can't, the road grader, the water truck, the dump truck, the blue rig truck, the tractor with shovel and two sets of power take-off, the backhoe, the four-wheeler. Then there are the machines directly used with these—the power winches on the front of both pickups, the horse trailer, the large flatbed, the platform saw and the drilling rig with high-speed and low-speed cables. This last can't be separated from the blue truck which carries it.

My favorite machine is the saw with its 36-inch diameter blade and movable platform which allows you to cut up huge chunks of wood. When we need firewood for the cabin, for Margo's pottery shop or for the houses in town, we lift the saw up by putting a chain around it and attaching the chain to the shovel on the tractor. We take the saw down along the watercourse and set it up—there's a ten-foot-long hard rubber belt which attaches to one cylinder at the saw blade and a second cylinder at the power take-off of the tractor. The tractor engine then becomes the power turning the saw blade.

Once the saw is set up we use the winch on one of the pickups to drag cottonwood branches up out of the watercourse. Wind, snow, ice, lightning—they all tear the trees apart. Small branches, large branches. Sometimes an entire tree comes down. Spring flood carries all these bits of wood until they're hopelessly tangled, a clotted jumbled mass.

To get the wood out, we set chokers around carefully selected logs and use the winch to pull. It's like the game we played as kids—pick-up sticks—only here instead of getting one stick without moving any other, you want to tug at the one piece of wood that will cause all the other pieces to come free.

In addition to the large machines, there are the tools.

When I open the shop door, I face a long room filled to overflowing with various types and sizes of hammers, adjustable wrenches, box and open-end wrenches, pipe wrenches, screwdrivers, saws, knives, fencing pliers, files.

My favorite tools are those that we use to make other tools or to retrofit machines. These include pipe threaders and reamers, drills and punches, metal cutters, riveters, grinders.

From the shop I take what Simon and I will need for the day's work—nine lengths of new willow rod which at 12 to 15 feet per length will give us the 124 feet we need. I also take six lengths of used but good rod—mixed lengths, many of them having been cut before—and a box of 1⅞-inch neoprene leathers.

Once everything is loaded in the trucks, Simon and I set off. He drives the Ford and I follow in the rig truck. We head for the Hupp Draw mill way out east near Powder River. It's a long slow drive up into the Breaks, the trucks groaning as we cross sand then clay then rock. There's one particularly bad spot where the track is narrow and cocked off at the angle of the hillside. I always fear that the truck is going to fall over on its side and so I lean the opposite direction, my body somehow imagining that this will keep everything upright.

Driving very slowly from the buildings to Powder River, I saw before me a great fluttering. From a distance it seemed to be something bright, sparkling as it leapt unpredictably up and down from the ground to about ten feet in the air. As I got closer I saw it was a swarm of butterflies. Most of them were fluttering on the ground—pushing and shoving in the manner of a crowd at an accident that is serious enough to draw our attention but not so serious as to repel us. Now and again a cluster of butterflies would burst into the air, making a brief explosion of light and color.

I stopped the truck and got out. I'd never seen so many butterflies at one time. I'd never seen butterflies clustered so densely together. The colors shifted and changed as the butterflies moved. I watched the undulating mass for what seemed to be a very long time.

Finally, I began to walk closer. The butterflies didn't seem to be disturbed by me. In fact, they took no apparent notice of my approach, continuing to hover and cluster. As before, they exploded into the air in small groups then plummeted back to the ground, crowding together. I walked into the butterflies and knelt down. There were butterflies tumbling around my head, their velvety dusty wings gently brushing my face and hair. A few landed on my shoulders and folded their wings up above their bodies. The breeze made them rock back and forth next to my face. I put my hands in front of me and carefully parted the cloud, leaning over to look down into the main body of beating color.

The butterflies were clustered over a large wet mass of cow manure. I remained still and watched. There were more and more butterflies. Now they swirled around my face so that I could see nothing else. Now my shoulders were completely covered.

I stood up and the butterflies that stood on my body fell away from me and back into the air. I walked away, back to the machines and to my work for the day.

The Windmills

♦

There are nineteen water wells at Four Mile Ranch. Four of these wells now use submersible electric pumps with power from the grid to bring water from underground reservoirs to the surface. One well uses a similar submersible pump, but the electricity comes from two photovoltaic panels designed to deliver twenty-four volts of electricity. Fourteen mills bring water up using the energy of the wind alone. These fourteen are true windmills.

Windmills, which once were common throughout the arid West in both the Rocky Mountain and Plains States, are growing increasingly rare. Often as I travel I see a windmill tower with no head. Or I see a tower complete with its fan and blades but when I get close I see that the spinning fan is not connected to anything. The blades make a thin whistling but nothing more. No water is brought forth.

The windmill is an elegant machine. By elegant, I mean both simple and sophisticated.

The Aermotor Company manufactured windmills in

Chicago for many decades. Now new windmills are often manufactured in Argentina. Or one can buy a rebuilt Aermotor from Muller Industries in Randolph, Nebraska. As Muller reminds us, "the windmill provides a low-cost, low-maintenance, energy-efficient means of pumping water for livestock and personal use."

One late August day, Simon and I completely pulled the windmill in the River Pasture east of the cabin. It's a deep well—we lifted thirteen lengths of pipe and twenty sticks out of the ground. There were no breaks in any of the joints of either pipes or sticks but the mill didn't pump. The plunger valve didn't seat and neither did the check valve. Or maybe the plunger valve would seat but the leathers weren't sealing. We couldn't tell. Maybe the working barrel was worn enough to keep the valves from working.

Whatever was wrong, it was going wrong 250 feet down in the dark so we had to pull it all up just to look. The valves were in good condition—cups in the cages smooth and even, balls settling in with no light showing.

"Huh?" Simon and I said to each other, and put on a new 1⅞-inch working barrel, replaced the leathers with Australian neoprene ones. The Australians claim that neoprene leathers make a better seal than leather leathers and last at least three times as long. At $6.00 a synthetic leather, they better last a long time. We put the neoprene leathers on and the mill, which had been drawing a little water up, completely quit pumping.

The sticks hung up in the pipe as if the leathers were too large for the working barrel and were keeping the plunger valve from moving inside the pipe. But that was impossible. We'd put in a brand new working barrel ground exactly to

1⅞-inch and the neoprene leathers were equally brand new calibrated to slide freely while sealing a 1⅞-inch opening. Well, something was up because there was no water coming out of this well. And there was no time that day to pull the mill again so we left it not working.

The next day we went back and started over—separated the rods above ground from the sticks below, pulled the twenty sticks out of the hole, pulled the thirteen lengths of pipe, inspected the working barrel, the cups and cages, the leathers. I guess you could say we were given the opportunity to live yesterday again today. The only change we made was to remove yesterday's brand-new Australian neoprene leathers and replace them with Texas yellow leathers.

When we reassembled the mill using the Texas leathers, it brought water up at a rate of slightly over a gallon and a half per minute—plenty of water. Clearly, the neoprene leathers had been defective. But just to see, we decided to use them again. The next time we worked on the Hupp Draw mill, a very shallow well that we can pull by hand in only a few minutes, we used the "defective" leathers and—*voilá*— the mill pumped fine.

This is the kind of experience that makes me read with some suspicion Muller's statement that windmills are a "low-cost, low-maintenance, energy-efficient means of pumping water for livestock and personal use." In fact, I believe that the windmill is more a religious artifact than it is a water retrieval system.

I've often spoken of the idea that all religions offer us names that are not so much God as they are the masks of God—Jesus, Mary, Buddha, Vishnu, Aphrodite, Moham-med, Salmon, Buffalo. It was the mythologist Joseph

Campbell who popularized this idea of the mask of God and my thinking is much like Campbell's except that I'd say even God is a mask of God. I could write a poem about it:

> His name's a metaphor and disguise
> hiding God from prying eyes.

But this wouldn't be a very good poem. Moreover, it would suggest that God is behind the mask when what I mean is that the spirit exists beyond naming. I'd as well worship the parts of a windmill as the names of the divinity.

A complete windmill includes:

> motor with helmet
> tail vane spring
> pump rod
> pivot bolt for tailbone
> furl lever complete
> upper furl ring with arms
> brake apparatus
> tail buffer device
> mast pipe with base
> wheel arms with nuts
> complete tail
> fan sections
> wood furl handle

To tell you the truth I don't recognize all of these names.

Once, as Simon and I were coming back from working on the South Hay Draw mill, we stopped near the cabin and walked over the rise of land to look down on another mill.

"Whenever you're near a windmill," Simon often reminds me, "always stop. There's bound to be something broken needs fixing."

And, indeed, as we stepped over the rise and looked down on the windmill behind the cabin, we could see that the fan was spinning but the sticks weren't going up and down. We walked down to the mill and found that the sticks above ground had separated from those below ground. The nuts and bolts that had been used to connect the chain to both the polish rod and the wood rod had loosened over time until the nuts had fallen off and the bolts hung uselessly through the links of chain. As the fan blades had turned, the wood rod had continued to travel but since it had nothing to keep its motion truly vertical, it had thrashed back and forth as it went up and down. It was splintered and cracked from bashing repeatedly against the metal tower supports.

I've focused a good deal of my attention in this book on the ways in which a windmill doesn't work. Let me tell how a windmill does work. First there is the tower. In the old days, towers were built from wood. Now they are steel. They may be as short as twenty feet or as tall as sixty feet. At the top of the tower and attached to it is a square platform on which one stands to work on the windmill head. This platform is usually made of four pieces of narrow board—one or two inches thick by six, eight or ten inches wide. If you're lucky, the boards will be eight or ten inches wide rather than six. And they'll be two inches thick rather than one.

At the top of the tower is the stub tower, a short shaft on which is perched the head. The head is made up of a cast-iron well and a steel helmet. Under the helmet is an assortment of gears and rods, drive shafts, cotter pins, nuts and bolts. In the bottom of the cast piece is an oil reservoir. The lower gear wheels rest in the oil and as they turn they carry oil to all of the moving parts under the helmet.

It is the wind alone that keeps all this oiled machinery in motion. When the wind blows, it strikes the windmill fan. The fan is made up of many steel blades, each of which is bolted at an oblique angle onto the fan frame. The fantail, like the tail of a weather vane, forces the blades to face directly into the wind. The wind, as it strikes the blades, forces the fan to turn. The turning fan causes a shaft to rotate. This shaft causes the gears floating in the oil to turn. The rotating gears cause a steel rod to go up and down. The distance of this up-and-down motion is six to ten inches.

So there you have it—the entire machinery of the windmill is designed to use the power of the wind to effect one action—to translate the motion of a shaft spinning on its own center parallel to the plane of the earth into the motion of a rod moving up and down perpendicular to the earth.

That translation effected and the shaft moving up and down, we have the capability to bring water out of the earth.

Attached to the steel shaft below the windmill head is a wooden rod. This rod may be as short as eight feet long, or as long as sixteen feet. Below it is attached another wooden rod and so on until the rods near the earth.

Directly below these rods is a hole in the ground—the well itself. Our wells vary in depth from slightly under one hundred feet to three hundred feet. The average depth is a little under two hundred feet. Inside the hole in the ground is a six-inch diameter casing. Inside the casing is a three-inch diameter galvanized pipe. Inside the pipe is a series of willow sticks. Each willow stick is ten to twenty feet in length. At one end of the stick is a male threaded fitting; at the other end is a female threaded fitting. Each stick is threaded into the one below it.

The willow sticks go down inside the galvanized pipe until they reach water. The willow stick that comes out of the earth is attached to a solid steel rod—the polish rod. This rod is joined to the sticks that come down from the windmill fan. The two sets of sticks may simply be bolted together. Often though, it is a chain that links them. In the event that something goes wrong and one or the other of the sets of sticks can't move, the chain can then "give" so that the sticks aren't snapped in half.

Each section of galvanized pipe that houses the willow sticks is twenty feet long. These lengths of galvanized pipe are also threaded together.

The working barrel—a brass cylinder twenty-four inches long—is attached to the bottom section of pipe. At the bottom of the working barrel is a check valve. The check valve is a cage inside of which is a steel ball. The steel ball can float up and down. When the ball is at its lowest point it nestles into a finely ground open bottomed cup. Below the check-valve cage is a hollow shaft around which are three compression rings. Screwed onto the bottom willow stick is another of these check valves.

When there is no wind, all of these parts wait, motionless and still. When the wind blows, the willow sticks—from the translated action of the spinning fan—begin to go up and down. As the sticks rise, the steel ball in the upper check valve settles into its cup making a seal so that water cannot sink below it. The compression rings adhere to the sides of the brass working barrel so that no water can leak around the outside of the check valve.

Like certain other parts of life, this sounds much more complicated when written down than it really is. Imagine if I sent you a windmill in the mail with only written instructions as how to set up and operate it. Then imagine how much easier all of this would be if you simply came to visit me here in northern Wyoming and I took you to the ranch. There we would overhaul a windmill together and all of these words would be superfluous.

When Margo, Caitlin and I went for a vacation to southern Mexico, we were shocked by the subtropical climate. It was, by Wyoming standards, warm, even hot, year round. One day the mother of the family we were living with told us that she had decided to commit herself to a regular aerobic fitness program and so had purchased a cross-country ski machine. It was made in the United States and the instructions for assembling it had come in English only. She and the other members of the family had gotten together and tried to assemble the "ski fitness center." It was hard to figure out exactly what to do though. "The instructions are so difficult," the mother told me. She and her family had given up. "You are a native speaker of English," she said. "Could you help us?"

I couldn't make head nor tail of the instructions and, in the end, I simply took the machine completely apart, laid all of the parts out on the floor in front of me, and stared at them until they began to cohere. It took two tries but we got it together and now our friend Elvira in Morelia, Michoacán, is happily cross-country skiing in the upstairs TV room each afternoon while outside the bougainvillea bloom.

The casing, pipe and stick are all submerged in an underground pool of water. There is constant water pressure at every surface. When the stick rises, the steel ball in the upper check valve is forced by gravity and the weight of the water above it to fall into the cup. Its downward escape impossible, the water must rise with the sticks.

Here comes what is for me the greatest part of the process. The wind continues to blow, the fan continues to turn, and the stick reaches the apex of its motion. It begins to move down. As it does, the ball in the bottom check valve rises from the pressure of water below it. This water pours into the working barrel. Now there's a six to ten inch column of water trapped between two check valves and being compressed as the willow stick journeys downward. The ball in the upper check valve rises from the pressure of the column of water below it and that short column rises into the galvanized pipe. With each up and down cycle of the willow stick, the narrow linked columns of water rise toward the surface—six to ten inches at a time.

I see I've explained this process three times. I'm unsure of my capability to make what happens clear. And each time I describe it, I'm amazed at the beauty and precision of the action, the magic of it.

It's a small bit of mechanical wizardry and one which pales beside greater scientific innovations—the internal combustion engine, the nuclear power plant, the silicon chip. And yet, these don't move me in the way of the check valve. Other small things also amaze me. This morning, for instance, I separated three eggs and beat the whites stiff to use in making waffles for my wife and daughter. It's a dazzling transformation. And bringing water up from hundreds of feet underground with no engines—unbelievable.

Perhaps it is that the smaller things seem to be less dangerous. I can't think of the internal combustion engine without thinking of the poisoning of our planet's air and water. It is the same with the waste from nuclear power plants. And nuclear power's less benign cousin, the nuclear weapon, brings nothing but destruction. And the silicon chip has brought us to the doorstep of an age in which there are no secrets, no privacy, no possibility of an individual life.

Yet the mind that gave us egg separation and windmills is the same mind that has given us nuclear bombs and computers. If that's true, then the joy I feel witnessing a windmill is the same joy I should feel when contemplating the splitting of the atom. I'm reluctant to accept this. Still, in the abstract, both are beautiful.

A few weeks after we had pulled the River Pasture East mill two days in a row, I went back to see if the mill was still working. I was worried as it had been so mysterious—pumping poorly, then not pumping at all and finally pumping very well. I didn't want to pull those 250 feet of sticks and pipes again.

When I got to the mill, there was no wind. I waited around and, after a few minutes, a light breeze came up. It was enough to turn the fan but not enough to really pump much. With a well 250 feet deep, it can take several minutes for water to appear. The lighter the breeze, the longer the wait.

I leaned down to the opening at the top of the pipe. I heard the familiar rattle of the check valve as the ball rolled up and down in its cage. I smelled the cold dark water, the traces of iron and soda. Suddenly the water tumbled out the end of the pipe and into the stock tank. I smiled.

I smile every time that first flow of water spills out. I am so happy to see the water and to think of how it comes to the surface, how the wind and the water are related to one another, how the water which shimmers in the light has waited so long in darkness. As the water fills the stock tank the sky is reflected there. And when I look down, my own face is reflected in the water, too.

In winter, this would all come to a grinding halt when the water froze. To keep the mill operating, there is, about six feet below ground in the top section of galvanized pipe, a hole smaller than the diameter of a five-penny nail. This is the bleed-back hole. Our frost level is about five feet—the ground freezes to that depth and so below five feet the water will not freeze. When the wind stops, the water in the top six feet of pipe drains out the bleed-back hole. When the wind blows again the mill can pump. Without a bleed-back hole, the water would freeze in the top section of pipe and then, when the fan began to turn, neither the rods nor sticks could. The fan, driven by the wind, would continue to turn and the sticks would break.

There must be a bleed-back hole if the mill is to pump in the cold. The chain that joins the upper and lower sticks is only an emergency backup device. If the bleed-back hole gets blocked and the water freezes in the pipe, the chain keeps the sticks from breaking until thaw. But that's all the chain can do. It can't bring water.

If the bleed-back hole is too big, the water runs out the pipe and back down the well faster than the mill can pump it up.

Each of us needs a bleed-back hole in our life. However strong we may be, we are also as fragile as a windmill. And we are at least as susceptible to freezing in winter. The tiny, seemingly inconsequential bleed-back hole keeps everything operable all through the winter. It's the most important part of the mill.

I step out into my garden in summer and it is as if I have stepped into Heaven. But the garden is not the bleed-back hole. The garden is everything else—gears and rods and oil and fans and check-valves.

Neither is the bleed-back hole my family—my wife and daughter—no matter how much I love them. This morning my daughter spent an hour being an octopus. She draped a yellow blanket over herself and told me she only had four limbs—the other four had been lost in a tragedy. She made jokes about her hard life, about how she must find her own home as her parent octopuses had died, about how she had come to spend the night with us but would stay longer to see what it was like here. At lunch time, she surreptitiously lifted the edge of her blanket to sneak a little food in. She said the blanket was her skin and her skin was her house. I watch her amazed, but she is not the bleed-back hole.

My wife's parents are loving souls who have given of themselves for me. Are they the bleed-back hole? What about community, justice, a glass of cool water on a hot day?

There is a small thing that will keep the channels open all year long. This small thing has two clear qualities: it is different for each of us and it resists being named.

These are the windmills of Four Mile Ranch along with their depths:

1. Morrison Pasture West: 236'
2. Morrison Pasture East: 190'
3. Bridge Pasture West—"Shorty": 140'
4. Bridge Pasture East: 180'

5. River Pasture Gas Plant: 180'

6. River Pasture Hupp Draw (way out east near Powder River): 90'

7. River Pasture Northeast of Cabin (you can see the Gas Plant mill from here): 231'

8. River Pasture East of Cabin (there are two ponds for this mill. My dream is to fence one pond so that cattle can't get to it. So I call this the Swimming Pool mill.): 250'

9. Behind Cabin: 190'

10. South Pasture West—the "Tangled Brake" mill (the brake cable repeatedly wraps itself around the pulley wheel and is cut, making it impossible to stop the fan from spinning in a wind. One of these days I'm going to get knocked into space by the fantail.): 168'

11. South Pasture Traud: 200'

12. South Pasture Big Reservoir: 215'

13. South Pasture South Hay Draw: 300'

14. Rickett's Field—formerly Harriets' Four Mile: 100'

15. Bridge Pasture New Electric: 130'

16. River Pasture near Gas Plant Electric: 180'

17. South Pasture near Cabin Electric—"El Relampago" (this mill has been struck by lightning several times): 220'

18. South Pasture North Hay Draw Electric: 160'

19. Four Mile Solar #1 – 380' of casing, pump at 60'

These windmills have given me water and something else, too. Not that they are the bleed-back hole, but they have shown me the way toward it.

Simon

♦

Because Four Mile is fairly large and because the windmills are spread over the entire ranch, we spend a lot of time driving to work. We have to take the rig truck in order to pull the pipe from the ground, or to lift the fan and head off. We take the Ford pickup with the flatbed box, too—it has the hand tools.

Sometimes when a tower has begun to slip into the ground and so must be straightened, we load the flatbed with bags and bags of ready-mix cement. We put the backhoe on a trailer and haul it behind the Ford to the windmill. After we unload the backhoe and unhitch the trailer, we drive the Ford back to the buildings to get the gold Jeep. We bring the Jeep to the mill and use its winch to pull the tower back to plumb and hold it in place while we repair the corner posts.

I have many times imagined the taut cable snapping and whipping through the air, slicing me in half.

After the tower is plumb, we dig a hole five feet deep around each corner and cement the tower in place—hand mixing the cement and shoveling it into the hole.

Sometimes as we're working on a mill, we discover a problem we hadn't foreseen and we have to drive back to the buildings for a part, or to jimmy doodle a temporary part until we can find the right thing.

The roads are dirt tracks, often little more than two faint shadows six or eight feet apart. Some of the roads are sand, some clay. In a few places, large jagged rocks fill the right-of-way. In spring, when it rains, the gumbo clay turns into a slick sheet—"slick as snot," they say. Then the way is nearly impassable. The wheels spin, the pickup wallows sideways. Great globs of clay are thrown up by the tires. The clay spatters the fenders, doors, windshield. It covers the mirrors. If the windows are open, it flies inside, splattering our clothing and faces. In summer the dust rises and is sucked into the cab of the truck nearly choking us.

The roads are best in winter when the earth is frozen and covered with hard-packed snow. But those conditions are rare. More often the wind has scoured the earth bare in one place while nearby there is a drift of snow rising like a wall before us. Simon usually tries to blast through the drifted snow. And usually we make it. Now and again we don't. In which case, we dig the truck out or we walk to get the other pickup to winch the stuck one out.

When we are riding together, going from one windmill to the next, or leaving the buildings to work, or coming back in the early evening, Simon often looks around and remembers out loud. Maybe we pass the site of a former spring, a caved-in dugout, a flat where bits of an abandoned wagon lie. Then Simon is telling me what happened and to whom. And so, slowly, in isolated bits and pieces, as the days gather, I am

learning the story of the ranch.

It is not exactly history as the telling is part fact, part dream, part longing, part resignation, part love and part resentment. The story is rich, full and present. In Simon's story there is only the perpetual now of Four Mile and those who have worked it.

After several years during which we have worked together on the two windmills in the Morrison Pasture, Simon tells me the pasture's story. The man who homesteaded this spot, and for whom the pasture is named, was Mr. Morris.

"If his name was Morris, why is this the Morrison Pasture?"

"We just call it Morrison 'cause it's easier to say. We've always called it that, even before it was part of Four Mile."

As we enter the pasture, there's a cabin made from rough-cut boards.

"Old Man Morris's place. For as long as I knew, he lived there alone, eating nothing but oatmeal and drinking nothing but coffee." Simon points up behind the cabin about a hundred yards where there's a slight oval depression and a few rotten fenceposts.

"That was the reservoir. He had it fenced so that the sheep couldn't get in. It was the drinking water for him and his horses—he didn't want sheep walking around in it, turning it into a mud bog. Old Man Morris lived in this cabin year round. He never bathed—put his winter clothes on in the fall and wore them until spring.

"During World War Two, when Morris was about seventy-five years old, the sheriff asked my dad to look after the old man. When I'd come back into town after work, I'd stop as often as I could to check on him. We had an old Ford pickup—this was before four-wheel drive, that didn't come till after the war, you know. One day I came slipping and sliding down here toward Morris's cabin. I spent the last half mile or so working on getting the truck stopped.

"I banged on the door but Old Man Morris didn't answer. I could see him through the one small window in the cabin. The window glass was always sooty and gray so Old Man Morris looked like a dirty, fire-damaged ghost. He was puttering around the stove, fussing with a few little sticks of cottonwood. I pounded harder on the door, then I shouted his name. I kept at it like that, pounding and shouting for a half an hour but he never heard me. He'd latched the door from the inside so I couldn't open it and stick my head in. Always latched the door, not to keep anyone out but to keep the wind from ripping the door open and off its hinges. I was about to give up and go when he opened the door to throw out a pail of dirty water. 'Hai, Simon, what are you doing there standing in the cold? You waiting for spring?' Then he laughed at me.

"He had an ear infection and couldn't hear so it didn't exactly matter what I answered. I motioned to him to ask how he was. He said fine. I asked him to come to town with me and have his ears checked but he refused. I kept asking and he kept refusing. When I turned to leave, he said, 'You better be careful, standing around the door to people's cabins, you're gonna get hit with a bucket of dirty water and froze to death.' I went on into Buffalo without him but told my dad and the sheriff about his ear infection. They came out and took Morris to the doctor who said the old man should stay in town for the winter. There was an ex-whorehouse that'd been made into a boarding house for elderly bachelors. 'Too bad,' is what Morris said.

"During that winter he spent in town, someone found his cabin, broke in and stole his saddle, tack, tools. Had to have been somebody local, nobody else would be out there. Cleaned Old Man Morris out. That was 1943."

When we come to Four Mile, it's usually by driving twenty miles out the Interstate to Schoonover Road and then twenty miles more generally southeast on the dirt county road to the ranch. Sometimes we come through the Morrison Pasture. We get off the Interstate at Dry Creek, turn onto Esponda's and past Bob and Jean Ruby's—I shouldn't say Ruby's as they've sold the place to a couple who are building two mansions and a horse barn more sumptuous than most people's houses. They're bringing in power, sinking wells.

I don't know these new owners but there is something about money that makes me nervous and fearful for this place—for Four Mile, for the small town of Buffalo, for Wyoming. And yet in comparative terms, as I said earlier, I am among the world's richest citizens.

At Ruby's, we cross Crazy Woman Creek and climb a steep ridge onto a sloping bench. We go southeast, the Bighorns shimmering behind our right shoulders. If it's anytime between September and June, the mountains will be covered by snow. In July and August, there will be only a few isolated patches of snow and, when viewed from the ranch, the mountains will look deep blue.

During the spring storm of 1984, it snowed continuously for the first five days of May. In town the drifts were fifteen feet high. The porch of our house was completely filled by snow. Margo and I opened the back door and began to dig the snow away, bringing it into the house and putting it in the bathtub where it melted and was later used to water houseplants.

After we'd carved out a small opening in the wall of snow, we began to shove lumps of snow forward. When the hole was large enough, Margo crawled out onto the porch just below the roof. I pushed her skis out to her, she strapped them on and, hunched over like a racer, she careened down the slope into the backyard and across the buried lawn to her pottery studio.

There were dead songbirds everywhere. They had already returned north and in a frenzied attempt to escape the storm had bashed themselves against the windows. Now they lay silently on the glittering snow. In death their color had left them. Even the crimson blood on their feathers had frozen to a dull brown. As the snow melted more dead birds appeared. Throughout that summer we found the occasional dead bird among the underbrush in the flower beds.

After that storm, half the sheep in the county were dead, and for several years there were no deer at Four Mile and only a few pronghorn. This year in early May, I saw ten pronghorn in the Morrison Pasture, and fourteen mule deer. There was a huge flock of tiny birds peeping and running furiously about near the Gas Plant well. I heard the meadowlarks calling off and on all day. A red-tailed hawk hung above the West Bridge mill.

The Bridge Pasture has its own little story—for years it was impossible to ford Four Mile Creek along a several mile stretch so Simon built a bridge. As soon as that bridge was finished, the creek stopped running and hasn't run since.

The bridge long ago rotted and has disappeared. We drive the trucks down the steep incline into the creek bed and then grind back out in four-wheel drive low. All that's left of the creek's water is the name Bridge Pasture. It's like the dikes in the hay draw—built those dikes and the water quit running.

The U.S. Geological Survey maps call the Hay Draw "Whiskey Draw," a name that's left from Prohibition. Now there's neither water nor whiskey, neither hay nor grain.

Four Mile is filled with little liquid problems and enticements. There are three fuel tanks behind the tool shop near the corrals. Each of these is operated with a hand pump. You pump the lever slowly and evenly up and down and the gasoline or diesel is forced out. But no matter how smoothly and evenly you pump, the gas comes out in a gushing spurt followed by a pause. The process is so slow that if you leave the engine running on some of the large machines they will burn fuel faster than you can put it in the tank. Four Mile's is a short history of liquid.

The Hupp Draw is named for Mr. Hupp. The draw is seven miles from the Four Mile cabin. To get there you rise with the land to the east, half-circle through a series of ridges, cross an expanse of boulders and sandstone and finally come down a steep narrow eroding hill into the draw, hidden at the bottom of a hole. It's hard to get in there now and would have been very hard indeed sixty years ago.

This is the spot where Mr. Hupp set up equipment to distill whiskey. It's far from the Whiskey Draw. But it's only a short distance to the water in Powder River and it's atop a coal bed Hupp used to make fire. When he finished the whiskey, he hauled it to town and sold it.

With the Ruby place well behind us, we keep moving

southeast along the ridge. There's a draw to our west, and on the next ridge past it there are a few scattered remnants of buildings.

"After the first World War, " Simon says, "there was a lot of homesteading in Powder River country. People thought they'd come out here and get their own place, be farmers. To the midwesterners the 640 acres they could get under the arid lands amendment to the Homestead Act sounded like a lot. They had no idea you couldn't make it with 640 acres. They tried dry farming and a lot of them, hardy souls, scrabbled by during the twenties, but there were those five or six years of bad drought in the thirties. Lot of people talk about how ranchers now have to have jobs in town to support their ranching habit. It was the same then—the men worked the oil fields down at Midwest, south of Kaycee. They'd be gone all week, the women doing all the work on the homestead. There was a one-room school on that ridge, had about ten students in the early thirties. By World War Two almost everyone had left to work in the shipyards on the Coast. The school was abandoned, but the building sat there on the ridge for years. I don't remember when it was torn down."

I look across the draw and think about that little community complete with its own school. Now it's just another ridge on Four Mile. Sixty years ago there were people all over this land.

Simon points out a piece of ground under a cutbank. "Four Basque bachelors each had a homestead there. You can see the corner where the four pieces met. Under the homestead law a person had to show that he was living on his land and that he was making improvements—buildings, fences. He had to do this in order to get clear title to the land after five years. These four Bascos built one cabin that sat on the four corner boundary. They lived together in the cabin and each one claimed it as an improvement on his homestead."

There are homestead remains all over Four Mile. In the Bridge Pasture there's a deep cistern near the watercourse. It's rocked in to slow seepage of water into the earth. We've covered the top to keep animals and people from tumbling in. Out near the West Bridge mill there's a dugout. The earth has collapsed on it, forming what looks like a miniature volcano. When I get down on my hands and knees and peer into the foot-high hole in the side of the earth, I can see that this is indeed human work. There are twisted cracked support beams and a litter of wood and metal on the earth. Simon counsels against going in as the whole thing may collapse.

"Someday I want to get the backhoe in here and open this up," he says, "See what's inside."

Out near the south boundary of the ranch is another dugout. And way out in the roughest barest land—the Breaks going toward Powder River—there's a spot on a ridge that's high and lonesome, commanding an open view of the Bighorns to the west and the jagged Breaks then prairie to the east. It was here that a homesteader ambitiously built a cabin and brought his midwestern wife to live.

His wife brought all her household furnishings and was aghast when she saw her new home. The cabin was several miles from the river so there was no water. There was no power and no road.

"That guy's wife wasn't very happy here." Simon says. "Finally, in a big wind, the cabin blew over and crumpled in a heap as it tipped over the edge of the ridge."

What's left is a smooth patch of black earth, sparkling

where there are bits of mica and granite, along with crushed china and crystal goblets.

Just before the Four Mile boundary coming in from Schoonover, there's a flat. Two bachelor brothers, Clyde and Ike Rickett, homesteaded here, and built their one-room cabin. "Clyde planted corn on the flat," Simon tells me, "and for years successfully raised his crop. He had no water for irrigation and there was no more rain on his cornfield than anywhere else in Powder River country. He planted in rows four feet apart, each plant several feet from the next. He cultivated the field several times each season and mulched around the plants. He fenced the field. Outside the fence the grass was burning up in the dry heat. But inside, his corn was deep green. You could hear the leaves rustling in the hot wind." As Simon speaks, I try to feel the cool life of the leaves pushing up and away, making a tiny convection current over the cornfield, a drift of air that is almost refreshing.

"Clyde had a two-horse team to pull a large heavy wheel that turned the earth between his wide corn rows. He spoke with a stutter and as he walked behind his horses he called to them, 'Hey, there, M-M-M-M-Maud, m-m-m-m-move along there, M M-M-M-Maud.'

"You could hear Clyde calling to Maud from up here at the Four Mile corrals, a mile from him and his brother Ike's fields." Simon pauses.

In *The Unknown Craftsman,* Soetsu Yanagi says, "Every artist knows that he is engaged in an encounter with infinity." Yanagi says that's what art is. It's what ranching is, too. Someone ought to write a book called *The Unknown Rancher.*

Simon speaks again. "Each brother had his own field.

Clyde's always did better. No matter how dry it was he somehow managed to get a crop of corn out of this soil."

I look at the open flat and try to imagine corn growing there. It's very nearly impossible to imagine it much less to have done it.

"Even though he knew how to survive here, Clyde left right after World War Two. That's almost fifty years ago, but you know, sometimes, I'll be up at the corrals working and I can hear Clyde calling out, 'Hey, M-M-M-M-Maud.'"

Simon turns and looks down on the airstrip flat below the fields. I've been with him enough to know that Dick Green homesteaded that spot. Dick had a suitcase of photographic negatives showing his homestead life. He'd taken pictures of everything—the building of his cabin, breaking the earth, planting and nurturing crops, his tools and machines, the cottonwoods along the watercourse, the hills. When Dick's cabin burned down, all those photographs, including the negatives, were lost.

In *This House of Sky*, Ivan Doig wrote: "Simply, it came down to this: homesteads of 160 acres, or even several times that size, made no sense in that vast and dry and belligerent landscape of the high mountain west. As well try to grow an orchard in a windowbox as to build a working ranch from such a patch."

So what if, I say to myself, you've got a landscape and weather as difficult as any Doig knew in Montana and people who not only don't have enough land to ranch, but are trying to farm! To farm where the precipitation may be sixteen inches a year, or twelve, or eight or six. Where the last frost will be in late May or early June. Where the first frost will be sometime in August, or maybe September if you're lucky. Where the summer highs will be over a hundred degrees and the wind will blow hot and dry, sucking the water out of everything. Where the winter lows will be twenty, thirty or forty below, bottoming out once in my memory at fifty-four below.

Then there's the wind chill. I remember a particularly cold spell one February when it went down to forty below night after night. One day it stayed cold and the wind came up. In town the bank near our house has a digital time and temperature sign. The banker often adds little notes congratulating people on their birthdays or anniversaries. Sometimes he puts a little joke on the digital readout. This day the sign read, "eighty below, ninety below, oh just forget it."

Well, Mr. Clyde Rickett was farming. He knew something about corn but he must also have known something about infinity and vision. I'd like to see Clyde and Soetsu Yanagi walking around here inspecting each corn plant, then looking up into the sky. Water and sky—the religion of life as it is.

Simon explains to me the importance of keeping sheep out of the new fresh succulent delicious sweet clover in Spring. He says, "There's nothing those sheep would like better than to eat that clover. But sweet clover is an anticoagulant. The sheep eat it, then you dock and when the knife takes that lamb's tail off, the blood gushes out. It's hard on most lambs, kills some of them. A lamb's not normally going to bleed to death from docking. But if they've been eating clover..."

One day when we went out to do some work, we found the dump truck had a dead battery. We wheeled the charger out from the tool shed and put it on the truck's battery. As we stood there, we saw that the cows had broken down the fence of the holding pasture to get to the hay stored there. They'd broken the fence in two spots and then managed to pull almost the entire thing down, trampling it and jerking barbed wire all over.

We'll put in new fenceposts and string new wire, and then we'll have a corral. But it'll be empty of feed, enclosing not hay but dust and cow shit.

On another day, we saw two pairs of mallards, one at the Hupp Draw mill then, later, one at the South Pasture West mill. I think they were the same pair—they'd flown ahead of us from Hupp to the South Pasture. At the South Pasture electric mill there were several killdeer, and nearby a sage hen. Skittering near the ground in front of the truck were hundreds of lark buntings, flying like a loosely defined single creature.

Until World War Two, work at Four Mile was done with horse teams. "My dad always had four, five or six work horses—big horses, eighteen to nineteen hundred pounds. Always had a few saddle horses, too. Didn't need them much, what with running a sheep operation."

That's about all Simon says about the transition from sheep to cattle. After the 1984 storm when so much domestic stock was killed, it cost more to buy a sheep than a person could make both from the wool and the sale of that same sheep. For Simon, the storm marked the end of sheep ranching. Four Mile became a cattle ranch, though not a cow-calf operation. That means cattle are not born and raised at the ranch. From spring through fall, Simon and I feed and water cattle. In the fall these cattle are weighed and sold and the following spring we bring in more calves.

These calves are owned by other ranchers who lease the use of Four Mile's grass. Sometimes we have been responsible for the total care of the cattle we are managing. Sometimes the cows' owners wish to take care of their stock themselves, in which case our responsibilities are solely ranch maintenance. We guarantee that fences, gates and cattle guards are in order. And we guarantee that there will be water for the cows to drink.

Simon often speaks of the days when Four Mile was a sheep ranch. He tells me that sheep were kept at the ranch throughout the winter. Winter work was mostly feeding those sheep. Twice a day hay and supplemental feed pellets—what we call cake—were hauled out and spread around for the sheep to eat.

"The hard part was water," Simon says. "Not just for the sheep, who can eat snow, but for the horses. All day I'd melt snow in a rendering kettle to make water for the horses to drink. Now, a horse out on winter range can get plenty of water from eating snow just like a sheep, but if that horse is working he needs more water than he can get from snow alone. I'd spend hours chopping sage for fire and filling a big cooking pot with snow. Takes a lot of snow to make a little water."

Those horses were hauling a sled, taking feed to sheep. Again and again, Simon tells me of the merits of sheep and the faults of cows. "In winter, a cow won't eat snow—you got to water that cow all winter long. Sheep'll get every bit of water they need from snow. And in spring they'll get water from dew. Think a cow would try that? No, sir." Simon's conclusion is, "There ain't an animal on this earth dumber than a cow, except maybe the man who owns one."

Simon and I have spent a lot of time repairing stock tanks. The traditional tank is a steel trough, either rectangular or circular, which sits on the ground. It's designed so that a cow can walk up to the tank, put its face in the water and drink. But that isn't what a cow does. If it can, a cow will walk right into the tank. And all cows bash the sides of the tanks, bend and break the bottoms. In an attempt to stop this damage, we build a fence around the tank which will allow the cow to get its head into the water but not its body into the tank. Our efforts rarely help though, as the cows shove on the fence until they break it and can wreck the tank.

Simon and I were out replacing a metal stock tank. It was before Simon had gotten the idea to use the giant tires from coal trucks. When we lifted the frail steel floor, we exposed a family of mice. Simon lifted his boot, as he had the first time we uncovered a bunch of mice, then he smiled at me. "Better save 'em for the eagles and owls, don't you guess?"

As a predator at the top of the food chain, I wonder a great deal about other predators and about the predator's role in the health of the biological web. The cruelty of it bothers me, and I don't understand it very well though I defend predators when ranchers say we need to get rid of them.

A fox or coyote may kill a lamb then bite through the lamb's side to eat the curdled milk in the stomach. Mountain lions will kill a lactating ewe and eat only the udder. Both bobcats and lions, after killing an animal, will drag the viscera away so as not to contaminate the meat. A coyote will break a lamb's neck and drag the animal away.

All of these predators will occasionally kill an animal and eat only the liver, kidneys and lungs. An eagle will pick up a lamb and fly away with it. What can the lamb be thinking as it disappears into the heavens?

Four Mile has a large prairie dog population. The prairie dog's natural predator is the black-footed ferret. The ferret is nearly extinct. It was, in fact, believed to be extinct until a small group was discovered near Meeteetse, Wyoming, in the early 1980s. Wyoming Game and Fish has been nurturing this ferret population in the hope of releasing substantial numbers back into the wild.

In the meantime, the prairie dog's most ardent predator is man. I say man meaning not human beings, but men— fat, thin, young, old, drunk, sober. A lot of men seem to love shooting prairie dogs for pleasure.

One day, leaving the ranch exhausted after working on a windmill we never got to pump right, we came upon two men and two teenaged boys leaning over the hood of a pickup. They cradled their rifles in their arms, firing fairly often, talking and laughing. Simon pulled up and rolled down the pickup window.

Nods all around. Silence. "How you doing?"

"We're target shooting prairie dogs," one of the men said, and one of the young boys went on, "Yeah, if you hit 'em right, they just explode before your eyes, like a watermelon." His eyes lit up and he explained how the pieces of prairie dog fly off in every direction. "Got to hit 'em right, though."

We went home. Simon said, "Not worth making a stink about."

Soetsu Yanagi said, "Seeing comes first. See first and know afterwards."

The difference between knowing the names of things and knowing the country. Knowing both how to take care of the earth and how to care for the earth. How is it that the fox biting through the lamb's stomach knows without knowing while the men and boys blowing up prairie dogs don't know while knowing?

I don't ask Simon that question. Everything I have observed of him over the years tells me that he is thinking about it and that, as yet, neither of us has the answer.

There's one last story. Each year in June the sheep were moved from winter pasture at Four Mile up to summer pasture in the Bighorns. The move took several days. Ranchers and herders walked slowly with the sheep, struggling to keep them together, to get them where they needed to be each night without frightening the spooky animals, without losing any of them.

"I was moving the sheep and my dad was going to come that night with food and water. I had a little bit of bread inside my shirt but it wasn't even really lunch just a snack. I was hungry. In the late afternoon, it began to rain hard. I was soaked, cold, hungry, tired. My dad never showed up. I got the sheep bedded down but couldn't sleep myself. I ate the bread then thought about all the huge dinners my mother had made for shearing crews over the years. I saw my dad sitting down to eat while I was miserable. The next morning my dad finally showed up and we had breakfast and I got dry clothes then it was time to move the sheep again. Ha! That's it."

"Ha! That's it." The closing words of Simon's last story. They're not much of an explanation of what has happened. There's a little postscript that comes after the last story that has helped me to make sense of Simon's "Ha! That's it."

Once, when we were working, Simon said he had a gift for me. He walked to the pickup and came back with a branding iron he'd come across, my initials with the D backed up against the R like this: ꓷR. It was an old brand—Simon had checked and found it was unregistered. "You oughta register it," he told me, "Never can tell when you might want to start a herd of your own." The iron was rusted and corroded, scarred by fire. Someone had used a hacksaw to cut about a third of the way through the lower loop of the D. The cut glowed red as if still hot.

What was the original brand for—Red Devil Ranch? Rocking Disaster? Dust and Rock? Or just Damned Ranch? How could Simon imagine I would ever have a herd of my own? Was he only making a joke?

The branding iron, like the stories, makes tangible something that is just beyond our ability to articulate, something that, though not invisible, is hard to see.

At Four Mile, the land and the air are filled with presences—the people who lived here before us, the pronghorn and deer, the coyotes and bobcats, our domestic cattle and sheep, the rocks and grass and cottonwood trees. You name it. We're not separate from these things, joining them only in the moment of death. Rather, we slowly get acquainted.

The years go by and Clyde and Ike Rickett are still dry farming corn, Maud still pulling. Dick Green is opening his suitcase of photographs. Mr. Hupp is pouring coal into the firebox of his still. Old Man Morris is living on oatmeal and coffee. Simon's mother is serving dinner to Simon's father and a shearing crew. After dinner they go back to clean the tools, check the cans of branding paint and begin again.

The ghosts, the land, the birds in the sky, the

subterranean water, an old branding iron, our memories—
they slowly fill us. One day they are us. We have been here
before; we just forgot.

Whatever we're doing, we've done it before and will do it
again. It's true of Four Mile and everywhere else—a little
joke life plays. But the joke doesn't have to be at our expense.
The windmills break; we repair them. They break again. We
repair them again and they break yet again and—Ha!—it's a
pleasure each time.